Bottle Collecting in America

Bottle Collecting in America

A Guide to Digging, Identification, and Pricing

A Companion Volume to *Bottle Collecting in New England*

John P. Adams

New Hampshire Publishing Company

Somersworth

1971

My heartfelt thanks to my family—to my wife Peggy and our two boys John, Jr. and Basil. The endless hours we've spent together photographing, cataloging, typing, and indexing have brought us closer as a family.

My thanks also to Tom Demerritt, Don Page, and Bob Filip for the hours we have enjoyed searching for and digging bottles and for the generous loan of some of their bottles, which helped make this book possible.

While the author appreciates hearing from other collectors about their experiences, he is unable to answer requests for appraisals or identifications.

Library of Congress catalog card number 70-151175

SBN 0-912274-06-9

Printed in the United States of America

Set in type by the New Hampshire Publishing Company. Bound by New Hampshire Bindery, Inc., Concord

The photographs on pages 9, 10, and 11 are by Bill Finney. All other photographs are by the author.

First Printing, February 1971

Second Printing, March 1971

Third Printing, April 1971

Fourth Printing, August 1971

Fifth Printing, June, 1972

Designed by David May

Contents

Two free-blown, open pontil, Persian Saddle-Flasks

Introduction

My feelings about bottle collecting haven't changed since my first book, *Bottle Collecting in New England.* I feel the same excitement when locating and digging a new dump. My family still participates in the early spring and late fall ventures, and the wonderful sights and smells of the woods and fields never fail to add to our enjoyment.

In this book I'll try to show you new ways of locating bottles, of trading, swapping, and purchasing from antique dealers. I have photographed more than 600 bottles and identified and priced them all. Except for those used to compare embossing and labels, hopefully no two are alike. A third book, containing another 600 bottles, is already being planned.

Letters from all across the country tell me of the excitement of digging, especially when the family joins together as a group. They confirm my feeling that doing things as a family can be the most rewarding moments in life. Parents state that in searching out and digging bottle dumps they have, for the first time in many years, truly experienced the thrill of being with their children. Teenagers and younger children write me as well, stating that they have rediscovered the joy of joining and working with their parents. And the many evenings spent together at home identifying and enjoying their finds bring further warmth to all members of the household. If you all participate in this uncommonly fascinating hobby, you will be amazed, I'm sure, by its dividends of knowledge and understanding.

Bottle collecting has so caught on that the uninitiated wonder: "Just what is this bottle mania! Why are people walking, camping, digging, and lugging in their pursuit of these hardened pieces of molten sand and chemicals!" I assure you that the reason is not monetary. When I first started searching for old bottles it was for the thrill of finding something old—something used, in most cases, over a century ago. You are literally digging up the history of our forefathers in what they drank and ate. Their illnesses are shown by the many medicinal bottles they used, and even those of their animals by the numerous "colic cures." Many medicines served a dual purpose, stating "good for man or beast."

Other items, now termed collectable, give us further knowledge. The many metal parts, at first undistinguishable in their ancient coat of rust, nevertheless many times tell us by implication so much about bygone lives. I once dug a free blown hatching egg and actually thought for a minute I had dug a preserved egg, it appeared so lifelike.

Many children's toys are excavated when searching for bottles, and these joyful objects of long ago seem more poignant when they are resurrected from oblivion and dust.

Not having dug bottles in all sections of the United States, I naturally cannot speak for every area, but I do believe that a strong feeling for the beautiful outdoors is common to every bottle digger. The many hours spent in nature, in this limited but vivid form of archaeology, do wonders for the person previously occupied with television and its shoddy simplifications. The beauty of the forests, the many different smells associated with nature, give one the feeling that he has missed something by not experiencing this sooner.

So bottle collecting is not just digging a bottle to add to your collection, but rather a return to nature, to the woods, fields, deserts, and mountains our forefathers originally contended with. It's a new awareness of what they suffered and died for, an indication of what they lived for. Some beginning collectors, too intent on finding that old mine's dumping location or deserted farm house or foundation that might produce additional bottles for their collections, might not at first be aware of these deeper feelings. But as they become more relaxed in their searching, taking time now and then to look around them, this latent feeling slowly, very slowly, begins to build up. The peak of excitement comes not in finding that rare bottle, but rather in finding yourself and nature together for the first time.

I practically grew up in the woods; as a child I frequently went with my father on long walks, hunting and fishing. I now trace my way back to all the areas we used to walk, the many deserted old farms I remember, the old roads that led to homesteads long since abandoned. I well remember the many bottles I broke as a boy, not knowing that some day I would be preserving them, not destroying them. How much greater is my excitement now, when with the eagerness of scientist and historian combined I search out the past.

All bottle collectors should be aware that, luckily, we are still living in an age when we can search for old glass containers and continue to dig them. How long this will last no one knows, but this is surely the golden age of our hobby, and in a disturbing world we should at least give thanks for this boon of enthusiasm.

John P. Adams

Dover, New Hampshire
January, 1971

New Techniques for Finding Bottles

Locating bottles was at one time a relatively easy chore. Because of the current interest in collecting by literally hundreds of thousands of people, old bottle locations are becoming scarce. There was a time when you could walk into an old area where people once homesteaded and, with a little searching, come up with a few choice bottles. Sometimes you were lucky enough to find a community dumping site and could lug away hundreds of old bottles and other glass and metal relics of bygone days.

Those days are slowly disappearing. There are, however, many dumps still to be found throughout the United States. Hardest to locate will be the few untouched dumping areas in the West, where bottle collecting started, but there are hundreds of spots in New England still intact. The southern states are just beginning to feel the excitement of discovering the beauty of old glass containers.

The oldest bottles will be found in New England, home of the early glasshouses. If you're from the West or South and are planning a New England vacation, I would recommend that you plan to search out old abandoned farm areas or visit antique shops, summer flea-markets, and bottle shows, where you may find some of the oldest and most beautiful bottles. I have found

Locating the dump site with the metal-detector

Pinpointing the spot and beginning to dig

the prices in New England to be very fair, sometimes much lower than you would find elsewhere. New Hampshire, for instance, is the home of many early glasshouses, and some of the most sought-after bottles were produced at the Stoddard and Keene glass works. As you travel throughout the state these particular bottles can be seen in many antique stores, shows, auctions, and flea-markets.

Maryland, Virginia, and the more southerly states are coming alive with finds of old bottles from farms and plantations. I have seen many of these bottles, and they are truly beautiful. I am impressed with the clarity of the bottles coming from the southern states. This may be due to less severe winters than New England and the northern states encounter; bottles exposed to greater temperature change deteriorate quicker.

With so many people digging and searching, roaming the woods and fields, deserts and mountains where mines and gold strikes once flourished, how can the average person find bottles? From experience I know that for nearly every dump area located on the surface or sub-surface there are several more well under the ground, out of sight of every digger. I therefore invested in a metal-detector, knowing that old glass was most always disposed of along with old metal. Because the detector sends out an audio signal, as well as having a readable needle, you quickly know when you move over metal. The detector is sensitive enough to locate a piece of metal the size of a dime six inches under the ground, and larger pieces as deep as six feet.

When I first purchased the detector I went back to the many dumps I had located over the years to see if I had missed any areas or could uncover new ones nearby. In these locations I had fairly well dug most of the bottles in the immediate vicinity. My return visits resulted in finding valuable bottles which I had missed earlier because they were not visible on the surface. The detector 'felt' the metal near the bottles under the surface.

Sand near ghost towns, ocean fronts where whaling once flourished, and mining camps are likely places to use the detector. Often the invisible lies only a foot or more under the surface. Although my main joy is locating old bottles, I also uncover many fine old metal parts. Those that are interesting and in not too bad a condition, I keep. These are usually old toys and farm imple-

Finding the first bottle

Many bottles later

ments, which I sandblast and coat with a rust preventative.

In searching for bottles with a metal-detector the most unlikely place often yields glass. I was crossing over a brook one day with the detector on and as I jumped the small bank I heard the audio signal. I didn't really believe it, so I jumped back again and the sound was repeated. The metal seemed to be located slightly under the stream bank. I dug and found a dump which eventually produced about fifty bottles. As I viewed the area, trying to reason how the dump got there, I finally realized that snow, ice, and erosion from a nearby incline had carried yesteryear's trash to the edge of the stream, which lay in a ravine, and nature's growth of a hundred years had imprisoned it at the brook's edge.

I reasoned also that perhaps some bottles had been carried downstream over the years. Additional searching with the detector for a distance of over two hundred yards down river produced at least a dozen more bottles lying directly in the stream bed under a layer of sand. None of these bottles would have been found had I not used the metal detector.

I purchased a unit that you assemble yourself, thereby saving about fifty per cent of the cost. As long as directions are followed, assembly is relatively simple. I honestly feel that a metal detector is a must for any serious collector, and for the investment he will be more than repaid during the first year's use.

Packing up for the trip out

An arrangement of medicinals

How, Where, & What to Buy

Perhaps the only way to add to your collection, outside of digging or trading, is purchasing bottles through the many club auctions, flea-markets, and antique shops in your area. Experience has shown me that regional bottle shows are the best source for buying otherwise hard to find bottles. Many of the bottles photographed in this book have been purchased through such local shows. The inexperienced collector should not purchase the more expensive bottles until his knowledge has grown.

Many persons start out taking nearly every bottle they come across in a dump as long as it is old. As you progress over the years you naturally become more selective, and the bottles you lug from a digging site become fewer. When you do become selective, it might be a good time to ask yourself some important questions. One might be just how many bottles you are going to collect. Is there a stopping point? Do you want to start a series or specialized collection? These are the questions I've had to ask myself. My game room has long since been filled. I have run out of space in my cleaning area. The many shelves I constructed had bottles waiting to be placed on them the moment they were finished, and my experiment of placing bottles in different areas on the main floor of our home to kind of "find another resting place" hasn't worked too well when my wife finds they need dusting. So, what to do? Well, I could move to a larger house—but heavens, can you imagine packing all those bottles? I've found that my answer is not only to be more selective but to select types of bottles I'm fond of and keep my eye open for these at the bottle and antique shows. I personally like sarsaparillas, inks, and miniature sample bottles, and I've found that the search for these specific types, or even for a specific bottle, heightens the excitement of collecting.

At the bottle shows and sales, most sellers hope you will "dicker" or barter with them. At the eastern shows, many dealers place cards on their tables with the bottles which simply state, "we like to dicker." This gives the limited-budget buyer a chance to stretch his dollars and come home with more bottles than he thought he could afford. The seasoned buyer knows what a bottle should be selling for and always hopes to purchase it at a lower cost. This 'dickering' back and forth between buyer and seller is one of the many exciting extras of bottle collecting.

If you handle bottles, whether at the bottle shows, antique shops, or flea-markets, always be prepared to pay for any bottle you may accidentally drop. At one show recently, I stood beside a man who had just picked up an historical flask priced at $90.00. He dropped it, narrowly missing my (I almost wish it had hit my toe if I could have saved the bottle), and it smashed on the cement floor. He very calmly took out his wallet, produced four twenties and a ten, and departed without a word. If you cannot afford to pay for a bottle, do not handle it more than is necessary.

Sometimes, while travelling out-of-the-way roads, you come across small family antique shops, which most often have bottles for sale. Some good purchases can be made by carefully looking around the barn or shed or wherever they have their shop. Some shops are nothing more than a table on the front lawn with bottles and other items for sale. Many times they will have a box or bushel basket with what appears to be low priced and dirty bottles, mostly clear glass with little embossing. From these "dollar" baskets I have found the following: one rye sunburst clear whiskey; several clear and aqua whiskey samplers; a brown cone ink; many ground top mason jars; and some beautiful insulators.

So keep your eyes open. Don't be afraid to climb a rafter in a barn if you see some bottles sitting on it, even if the dealer says, "Oh, those. Been up there for years—not worth much." I climbed a ladder to such a rafter and found a black glass whiskey sampler with the original label and contents. I asked the dealer what he wanted for it, and he said, "Oh, two dollars will do." Which I gladly paid.

Another such episode didn't pan out as well, but I was glad at least I had helped the shop owner discover some bottles he didn't know he had. I had spotted some bottles on a rafter and after the owner and I found a ladder I climbed up to them. While looking I noticed some boxes partially open and from where I was I thought I could see some bottle tops. I crawled over and found two boxes of old whiskey bottles with labels attached. The shop owner, having recently purchased the farm, hadn't known they were there. He logically wanted to research the bottles for value before he sold them, but he did give me first option.

As bottle enthusiasts grow in number, and dumps become scarce, you should investigate other ways of procuring bottles at little or no cost. I find that I constantly dig up duplicate bottles. I clean these and put them aside, and when I go bottle shopping I take them with me for trading. Dealers, as you know, naturally have to make a profit. You wouldn't have a shop to go to if they didn't. Therefore remember this when you trade. Don't expect to swap even, but give a little in your dickering. Perhaps, if you can't come to an agreement, a dollar or two will break the deadlock.

Be it buying, trading, or selling, however, do it for enjoyment and not for material gain, for this is the greatest gift you will receive from that thing called "bottle mania."

Identifying & Pricing

Identification of old bottles can be as exciting as digging itself. After cleaning my bottles from past diggings, I catalog each one. That is, I measure it for height, record color and embossing, note what it contained and how it was made. If your question now is, "Where do I locate all that information?" let me go back six years.

When I first started digging, one of the most difficult things about bottle collecting was identification. At the time I had few books and knew fewer people interested in bottle collecting. One of my first purchases was a book containing graphic outlines of bottles taken from old glass and bottle manufacturing catalogs. The illustra-

tions clearly showed the outline of the bottle and told what it contained. Naturally this book could not possibly show every bottle made—nor can any book, for that matter.

Over the years, as I purchased other books, talked with collectors, and visited bottle shows and antique shops, I increased my knowledge to the point that very few bottles I dug stumped me. It's nice to be able to dig and identify at the same time, but when I come across an unknown bottle I have to admit it is exciting to know that I will have to do some research in order to identify it. I still have a few bottles today which I have not yet identified. I constantly keep an eye open at shows and shops in hopes I will find similar

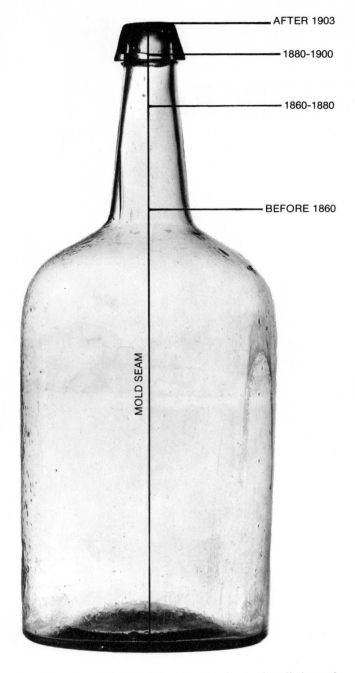

AFTER 1903

1880-1900

1860-1880

BEFORE 1860

MOLD SEAM

Age Gauge: *The bottle shown is a demijohn of 1860-1880 vintage with applied lip and is used only as an illustration showing height of seam with corresponding year.*

ones, but with labels which will give me an identification of what my bottles contained.

Here are some ways to gain knowledge about identification.

1. Read as many different books as possible pertaining to bottles.
2. Visit museums or restored colonial areas where most old bottles are labeled and identified.
3. Research in libraries for books pertaining to glass and old glass factories.
4. Talk with fellow collectors.
5. Visit with antique dealers wherever you travel; this will give you indications of price variations in various states.
6. Go to local so-called 'flea markets' and auctions.
7. Join your local bottle club; if there isn't one in your area get a group together and start one.

Everyone wants to know the value of the container he has found. Besides the seven listed "rules" for identification, you should add a little something called feeling. When I say feeling I do not mean placing a high value on your find because you got stung by a hornet or suffered a bad case of poison ivy, or even walked seven miles and came back with only one bottle! All of these have happened to me—and more. What I do mean is a feeling towards the particular bottle for its embossing, shape, or design. Is the neck bent? Is the lip applied crudely or sloping? Is it a free-blown with a rough pontil? Is it of clear glass, beautiful at times with its tinges of sun-colored amethyst, or is it of deep cobalt blue, gold, peacock blue, or emerald green? All of these are factors in pricing your bottle. If you are tempted to sell or trade but are in doubt as to value, hold off, for there is nothing more heartbreaking than to sell a bottle for a few dollars only to find later it was rare and worth ten times that. I do, however, have one rule I follow and that is, be fair with people and they will be fair with you.

600 Bottles

PHOTOGRAPHED, PRICED,

AND IDENTIFIED

All bottles are shown approximately one-half actual size.

Captions reading from top to bottom describe bottles from left to right.

Abbreviations

B.I.M.   Blown in mold

S.C.A.   Sun-colored amethyst

A.B.M.   Automatic bottle machine

EMBOSSING	HEIGHT	TYPE	COLOR	HOW MADE	PRICE
NONE	10 ¾	Taper Gin	Dark Olive	B.I.M. Whittle Marked	8.00–10.00
VERONICA MEDICINAL SPRING WATER	10 ½	Mineral Water	Amber	B.I.M.	4.00–5.00
NONE	10	Unknown (possibly gin)	Gold	B.I.M.	6.00–8.00
NONE	10 ⅛	Taper Gin	Olive	Free Blown Open Pontil Whittle Marked	25.00–30.00

EMBOSSING	HEIGHT	TYPE	COLOR	HOW MADE	PRICE
NONE (design as shown)	11 ¾	Unknown	Clear	B.I.M.	6.00–7.00
HARVARD RYE (design as shown)	11 ¾	Liquor	Clear	B.I.M.	6.00–8.00
H. W. HUGULEY CO. 134 CANAL ST. BOSTON	11 ⅜	Whiskey	S.C.A.	B.I.M.	4.00–5.00
NONE (design as shown)	11 ¼	Whiskey	Clear	B.I.M.	7.00–9.00

EMBOSSING	HEIGHT	TYPE	COLOR	HOW MADE	PRICE
WRIGHT & TAYLOR DISTILLERS LOUISVILLE, KY. REGISTERED on back: FULL QUART	9 ½	Whiskey	Brown	B.I.M.	6.00–8.00
NONE	9 ½	Squat Brandy	Amber Brown	Turn Mold	3.00–4.00
WRIGHT & TAYLOR DISTILLERS LOUISVILLE, KY. on back: FULL QUART REGISTERED	9 ½	Whiskey	Brown	B.I.M.	5.00–7.00

EMBOSSING	HEIGHT	TYPE	COLOR	HOW MADE	PRICE
NONE	10 ½	Ale	Olive	Three-Piece Mold Whittle Marked	5.00-7.00
NONE (paper label as shown)	9 ⅞	Gin	Dark Olive	Three-Piece Mold	6.00-8.00
NONE	10 ½	Ale	Olive	Three-Piece Mold Whittle Marked	5.00-7.00
NONE	11 ½	Whiskey	Teal Green	Three-Piece Mold Whittle Marked	8.00-10.00

EMBOSSING	HEIGHT	TYPE	COLOR	HOW MADE	PRICE
CUCKOO WHISKEY REX DISTILLING CO. BOSTON, MASS. on back: FULL QUART (mono as shown)	11 ¾	Whiskey	Clear	B.I.M.	5.00-7.00
SUNNYSIDE WHISKEY SAMPLE & CO. NEW YORK (gold leaf embossing)	11 ¼	Whiskey	Clear	Turn Mold	6.00-8.00
NONE (paper label as shown)	11 ¾	Whiskey	Clear	B.I.M. Three-Piece Mold	2.50-3.50
NONE	12 ½	Whiskey	S.C.A.	B.I.M.	3.00-4.00

EMBOSSING	HEIGHT	TYPE	COLOR	HOW MADE	PRICE
NONE	12	Liquor	Dark Olive Green	Turn Mold	3.00-4.00
CHARLES & CO. NEW YORK	11 ¾	Whiskey	Red Amber	B.I.M.	5.00-7.00
NONE	11 ¼	Liquor	Olive Amber	Three-Piece Mold	3.00-4.00
NONE	12	Wine	Olive Green	Turn Mold	2.50-3.50

EMBOSSING	HEIGHT	TYPE	COLOR	HOW MADE	PRICE
NONE (label as shown)	11 ¾	Grape Brandy	Amber	Three-Piece Mold Whittle Marked	7.00-9.00
NONE	11 ¼	Brandy	Light Olive Green	Three-Piece Mold Whittle Marked	6.00-8.00
NONE	11 ⅛	Brandy	Gold Amber	Three-Piece Mold Whittle Marked	6.00-8.00
NONE	11 ¼	Whiskey	Amber	Turn Mold	3.50-4.50

EMBOSSING	HEIGHT	TYPE	COLOR	HOW MADE	PRICE
NONE (paper label as shown)	11 ¼	Gin	Light Green	Three-Piece Mold Whittle Marked Glass Stopper	3.00–4.00
NONE (squat seal as shown)	9 ⅝	Brandy	Clear	B.I.M.	2.50–3.50
ESTABLISHED 1851 TRADE MARK OPTIMA SATIS BONA EST W.M. JONES AND CO. BOSTON (figure as shown)	9 ⅜	Whiskey	Clear	B.I.M.	3.00–4.00
POLAND WATER H. RICKER & SONS' PROPRIETOR'S POLAND MINERAL SPRING WATER on back: initials and seal	11 ⅛	Mineral Water	Clear	B.I.M. Whittle Marked	7.00–9.00

EMBOSSING	HEIGHT	TYPE	COLOR	HOW MADE	PRICE
NONE	10 ¼	Brandy	Olive Green	B.I.M.	4.00–6.00
THE HAYNER DISTILLING CO. DAYTON ST. LOUIS ATLANTA ST. PAUL DISTILLERS on base: DESIGN PATENTED NOV. 30th 1897	11 ⅝	Whiskey	Clear	B.I.M.	4.00–6.00
HAYNER WHISKEY DISTILLERY TROY, OHIO on base: DESIGN PATENTED NOV. 30th 1897	11 ⅜	Whiskey	Clear	B.I.M.	4.00–6.00
on base: DYOTTVILLE GLASS WORKS PHILa	11 ¼	Whiskey	Olive Gold	B.I.M. Graphite Pontil	25.00–30.00

EMBOSSING	HEIGHT	TYPE	COLOR	HOW MADE	PRICE
(paper label as shown) on base: REGISTERED G.O. TAYLOR TRADE MARK	11 ⅜	Bourbon	Amber Gold	B.I.M. Three-Piece Mold	5.00–6.00
NONE on base: four flowered petals	9 ¾	Taper Gin	Olive	B.I.M.	7.00–9.00
NONE	9	Taper Gin	Clear	B.I.M.	3.00–5.00
(paper label as shown) on back: WARNER'S SAFE KIDNEY & LIVER CURE ROCHESTER, N. Y. (mono of safe with words TRADE MARK)	9 ⅜	Medicinal	Amber	B.I.M.	12.00–15.00

EMBOSSING	HEIGHT	TYPE	COLOR	HOW MADE	PRICE
NONE	11 ½	Brandy	Plum	Three-Piece Mold	15.00-18.00
NONE	11 ⅜	Brandy	Amber Brown	Three-Piece Mold Ground Pontil Whittle Marked	8.00-10.00
NONE on base: stoddard X	11 ½	Brandy	Amber	Three-Piece Mold Whittle Marked	6.00-8.00
NONE	11 ¾	Whiskey	Olive Green	Three-Piece Mold Whittle Marked	6.00-8.00

EMBOSSING	HEIGHT	TYPE	COLOR	HOW MADE	PRICE
F. MANNS ROOT BEER	10 ⅛	Beverage	Light Brown	Pottery	4.00-5.00
NONE	11 ¼	Wine	Clear	Turn Mold Push Up	2.50-3.50
NONE	11 ¼	Beverage	Brown	B.I.M.	2.50-3.50
THE HAYNER DISTILLING CO. DAYTON ST. LOUIS ATLANTA St. PAUL DISTILLERS on base: DESIGN PATENTED NOV. 30th 1897	11 ⅝	Whiskey	Plain	B.I.M.	4.00-6.00

EMBOSSING	HEIGHT	TYPE	COLOR	HOW MADE	PRICE
NONE	12 ⅛	Wine	Light Blue	B.I.M.	4.00-6.00
NONE	12	Wine	Clear	B.I.M.	1.50-2.50
NONE (swirls as shown with glass stopper)	10 ⅞	Brandy Decanter	Clear	B.I.M.	12.00-15.00
NONE	12	Wine	Yellow Green	B.I.M. Whittle Marked Push Up	4.00-6.00

EMBOSSING	HEIGHT	TYPE	COLOR	HOW MADE	PRICE
TRADE MARK THIS BOTTLE IS NOT SOLD BUT REMAINS PROPERTY OF SIR. R. BURNETT & CO. LONDON ENGLAND (mono as shown)	12	Gin	Aqua	B.I.M. Glass Stopper	3.50-5.00
ARRAKS PUNSCH	11 ⅝	Wine	Aqua	Turn Mold Push Up	3.50-5.00
NONE	11	Cordial	Clear	Turn Mold	3.00-4.50
(half moons as shown)	11 ¼	Brandy	Clear	B.I.M.	3.00-4.50
FISHER & FAIRBANKS BOSTON, MASS. on back: mono	12 ¾	Unknown	Aqua	B.I.M.	4.00-6.00

EMBOSSING	HEIGHT	TYPE	COLOR	HOW MADE	PRICE
NONE	16 ½	Cordial	Clear	Turn Mold	2.50-3.50
NONE	16	Hock Wine	Teal Blue	Turn Mold	10.00-15.00
DITTA G. ALBERTI BENEVENTO (sun as shown)	12 ½	Cordial	S.C.A.	B.I.M.	6.00-8.00

EMBOSSING	HEIGHT	TYPE	COLOR	HOW MADE	PRICE
NONE	14	Hock Wine	Amber	Turn Mold	4.00-6.00
L. ROSE & CO (flowers as shown)	14	Limewater	Aqua	B.I.M.	6.00-8.00
NONE	13 ¼	Hock Wine	Aqua	B.I.M.	2.50-3.50
NONE	13 ¾	Hock Wine	Amber Gold	B.I.M. Whittle Marked	6.00-8.00

EMBOSSING	HEIGHT	TYPE	COLOR	HOW MADE	PRICE
WHITE HORSE WHISKY	10 ¼	Whiskey	Olive Green	Three-Piece Mold Whittle Marked	5.00-7.00
LASH'S KIDNEY AND LIVER BITTERS on back: THE BEST CATHARTIC AND BLOOD PURIFIER	9 ¼	Bitters	Brown	B.I.M.	8.00-10.00
NONE (paper label as shown)	9 ⅛	Medicinal	Brown	A.B.M.	1.50-2.50
NONE	9 ¼	Taper Gin	Olive Amber	B.I.M.	7.00-9.00

EMBOSSING	HEIGHT	TYPE	COLOR	HOW MADE	PRICE
NONE	10 ⅞	Whiskey	Gold Amber	Three-Piece Mold	4.50-6.50
NONE	10	Medicinal	Aqua	Three-Piece Mold Open Pontil	8.00-10.00
NONE	10 ⅛	Olive Oil	Aqua	B.I.M.	3.50-4.50
MOXIE NERVE FOOD LOWELL, MASS.	10	Medicinal	Aqua	B.I.M. Whittle Marked	4.00-6.00
MOXIE NERVE FOOD LOWELL, MASS.	10 ¼	Medicinal	Light Aqua	B.I.M. Whittle Marked	4.00-6.00

EMBOSSING	HEIGHT	TYPE	COLOR	HOW MADE	PRICE
NONE (paper label as shown)	12	Food	Green	Turn Mold	2.50–3.50
NONE	11 ½	Beverage (possibly grape juice)	Green	Three-Piece Mold	2.00–3.00
NONE	11 ⅞	Beverage	Amber Brown	Turn Mold	2.00–2.50
NONE	11 ⅝	Wine	Olive Green	Free Blown Open Pontil	20.00–25.00

EMBOSSING	HEIGHT	TYPE	COLOR	HOW MADE	PRICE
SCHIEDAM UDOLPHOWOLFE'S AROMATIC SCHNAPPS	9 ⅜	Medicinal	Light Olive	B.I.M. Ground Pontil	10.00-15.00
PROPERTY OF ROCHESTER BREW. CO. BOSTON BRANCH 95	9 ⅜	Beer	Amber Brown	B.I.M.	3.00-4.00
NONE	9 ⅝	Wine	Light Olive Green	Turn Mold	2.00-3.00
NONE	9 ¾	Ale	Olive Green	Turn Mold	2.50-3.50
on base: M C R CO. BOSTON	9 ½	Taper Gin	Olive	B.I.M.	7.00-9.00

EMBOSSING	HEIGHT	TYPE	COLOR	HOW MADE	PRICE
THE DUFFY MALT WHISKEY COMPANY BALTIMORE MD. U.S.A. (mono as shown) on base: PAT AUG 24 86. BALTIMORE MD.	10 ¼	Whiskey	Amber	B.I.M. Whittle Marked	6.00-8.00
THE DUFFY MALT WHISKEY COMPANY ROCHESTER, N. Y. U.S.A. (mono as shown) on base: PATd AUG. 24 1886	10 ¼	Whiskey	Brown	B.I.M.	5.00-7.00
NONE	8 ⅜	Medicinal (tablets)	Cobalt Blue	B.I.M.	3.00-5.00
Dr J. HOSTETTER'S STOMACH BITTERS	8 ¼	Bitters	Amber	B.I.M.	8.00-10.00
Dr J. HOSTETTER'S STOMACH BITTERS on base: 7 L & W	9	Bitters	Brown	B.I.M.	8.00-10.00

EMBOSSING	HEIGHT	TYPE	COLOR	HOW MADE	PRICE
NONE	7 ½	Ale	Olive	Free Blown Ground Pontil Whittle Marked	10.00-15.00
NONE	9 ¼	Ale	Brown	B.I.M. Whittle Marked	4.00-5.50
NONE	9 ⅜	Taper Gin	Green	B.I.M. Whittle Marked	16.00-20.00
NONE	9 ¼	Ale	Amber Brown	B.I.M. Whittle Marked	4.00-6.00
NONE	8 ¼	Ale	Olive	Free Blown Ground Pontil	12.00-18.00

EMBOSSING	HEIGHT	TYPE	COLOR	HOW MADE	PRICE
NONE	7 ⅝	Whiskey (union oval flask)	Gold	B.I.M. Strap-Sided Whittle Marked	8.00-10.00
JUAN DIEGO MADE IN MEXICO NS DE GUADALUPE (figure as shown)	5 ½	Commemorative Flask	Amber Gold	Open Pontil Whittle Marked	25.00-35.00
NONE	7 ½	Pint Stoddard Whiskey Flask	Deep Amber	B.I.M. Whittle Marked (Stoddard, N. H., Glass Works)	30.00-40.00
32 OZS. CONTENTS	9 ⅝	Whiskey	Green	B.I.M. Strap-Sided	8.00-10.00

EMBOSSING	HEIGHT	TYPE	COLOR	HOW MADE	PRICE
NONE	8	Whiskey (Picnic Flask)	Clear	B.I.M.	4.00–6.00
NONE	9 ⅝	Whiskey (Union Oval Flask)	Gold	B.I.M. Strap-Sided	8.00–10.00
C. H. GRAVES & SONS BOSTON, MASS. STANDARD FOREIGN & DOMESTIC SPIRITS	8 ½	Liquor	Clear	B.I.M.	3.50–4.50

EMBOSSING	HEIGHT	TYPE	COLOR	HOW MADE	PRICE
NONE	6 ⅛	Half Pint Stoddard Whiskey Flask	Amber Gold	B.I.M. Whittle Marked (Stoddard, N. H., Glass Works)	40.00-50.00
PATENT	6	Half Pint Stoddard Whiskey Flask	Deep Olive Amber Gold	B.I.M. Whittle Marked (Stoddard, N. H., Glass Works)	45.00-55.00
NONE (faint seal on face)	7 ⅞	Whiskey	Gold	B.I.M.	15.00-18.00
NONE	9 ½	Whiskey	Amber	B.I.M. Strap-Sided	6.50-8.50

EMBOSSING	HEIGHT	TYPE	COLOR	HOW MADE	PRICE
NONE	7 ⅝	Whiskey (Shoo Fly Flask)	Aqua	B.I.M.	4.00–6.00
NONE (design as shown)	6 ⅝	Whiskey (Picnic Flask)	Clear	B.I.M.	8.00–10.00
NONE on base: AYER	7 ½	Cosmetic (Hair Tonic)	Aqua	B.I.M. Whittle Marked	2.00–2.50
HOYT BROTHERS WHOLESALE LIQUORS 49 WASHINGTON ST. LYNN, MASS. on back: H B	7 ⅜	Whiskey	S.C.A.	B.I.M. Strap-Sided	3.50–5.50

EMBOSSING	HEIGHT	TYPE	COLOR	HOW MADE	PRICE
NONE	9 ½	Whiskey (Union Oval Flask)	Clear	B.I.M. Strap-Sided	3.50–4.50
THE WORCESTER D & R FLASK TRADE MARK	8 ⅛	Whiskey (Union Oval Flask)	Clear	B.I.M. Strap-Sided	4.00–5.00
NONE	7 ⅝	Whiskey (Union Oval Flask)	Aqua	B.I.M. Whittle Marked Strap-Sided	4.00–6.00
HOWELLS CELEBRATED AMMONIA	9 ⅛	Household	Aqua	B.I.M.	3.00–4.00

EMBOSSING	HEIGHT	TYPE	COLOR	HOW MADE	PRICE
1 PINT	7 ⅞	Whiskey	Amber	B.I.M.	2.50-3.50
JOHN HAYES & CO MANCHESTER N. H. WHOLESALE DEALERS	6 ⅛	Whiskey	Gold Amber	B.I.M. Strap-Sided	7.00-9.00
NONE	6	Whiskey	Amber Brown	B.I.M. Strap-Sided Whittle Marked	5.00-7.00
NONE	7 ⅛	Whiskey (Shoo Fly Flask)	Amber	B.I.M.	6.00-8.00

EMBOSSING	HEIGHT	TYPE	COLOR	HOW MADE	PRICE
HYDROZONE PREPARED ONLY BY CHAS. MARCHAND NEW YORK U.S.A.	7	Chemical	Brown Amber	B.I.M.	2.50-3.50
Dr J G B SIEGERT & SONS on base: ANGOSTURA BITTERS	8	Bitters	Green	A.B.M.	3.00-5.00
NONE	8 ¼	Taper Gin	Olive Green	B.I.M.	8.00-10.00
on base: T. METCALF CO. BOSTON	7 ½	Medicinal	Brown Amber	B.I.M.	2.00-3.00
WARNER'S SAFE REMEDY 8 FL OZ ROCHESTER, N. Y. safe with words TRADE MARK	7 ¼	Medicinal	Amber	B.I.M.	10.00-15.00

EMBOSSING	HEIGHT	TYPE	COLOR	HOW MADE	PRICE
HENRY K. WAMPOLE & CO. PHILAD.	8 ⅜	Medicinal	Amber Brown	B.I.M. Whittle Marked	4.00-5.00
NONE on base: ARNAO 331	8 ⅛	Beer or Ale	Amber Brown	Three-Piece Mold Whittle Marked	4.00-5.00
NONE	8 ¼	Wine	Green	Turn Mold	2.50-3.50
JOHN WYETH & BRO. PHILADELPHIA	8 ⅞	Malt Extract	Amber Brown	B.I.M.	4.50-5.50
JOHN WYETH & BRO. PHILADELPHIA	9 ⅛	Malt Extract	Brown	B.I.M.	4.00-5.00

EMBOSSING	HEIGHT	TYPE	COLOR	HOW MADE	PRICE
BURKHARDT BREWING CO. BOSTON, MASS REGISTERED	8 ¼	Beer	Amber	B.I.M.	3.50-5.00
JOHANN HOFF	7 ¾	Malt Extract	Brown	B.I.M. Whittle Marked	3.50-5.00
C. W. ABBOTT & CO. BALTIMORE on base: C.W. ABBOTT & CO. BALTIMORE	8	Bitters	Brown	B.I.M.	5.00-7.00
NONE	7 ¾	Medicinal	Olive Brown	B.I.M. Stoddard Glass	7.00-9.00
JOHN WYETH & BRO. PHILADELPHIA LIQ. EXT. MALT	8 ⅞	Food	Brown	B.I.M.	4.00-5.00

EMBOSSING	HEIGHT	TYPE	COLOR	HOW MADE	TYPE
NONE	8 ½	Ale	Dark Olive Green	Free Blown Ground Pontil	12.00-16.00
NONE (paper label as shown)	7 ¼	Wine	Light Olive Green	B.I.M.	3.50-4.50
JOHANN HOFF	7 ½	Malt Extract	Olive	B.I.M.	3.50-5.00
JOHANN HOFF	7 ⅝	Malt Extract	Olive Green	B.I.M. Whittle Marked	4.50-5.50

EMBOSSING	HEIGHT	TYPE	COLOR	HOW MADE	PRICE
REGISTERED ROBINSON BROS. DOVER, N. H. (mono as shown)	9 ⅜	Beverage	Brown	B.I.M. Whittle Marked	2.50-3.50
NONE (paper label as shown)	9 ¼	Wine	Light Olive Green	Turn Mold	4.00-4.50
NONE	9 ⅞	Fire Extinguisher	Brown	B.I.M.	4.50-6.50
(initials JSP as shown)	9 ½	Food	Teal Green	B.I.M.	6.00-8.00
NONE	9 ½	Ale	Olive	B.I.M. Three-Piece Mold Whittle Marked	3.50-4.50
on base: E. & J. BURKE E J & B	10	Beverage	Olive	B.I.M.	2.00-3.00

EMBOSSING	HEIGHT	TYPE	COLOR	HOW MADE	PRICE
NONE	9 ¾	Wine	Olive Green	Turn Mold	2.50–3.50
NONE	9	Ale	Olive Green	B.I.M. Three-Piece Mold Whittle Marked Ground Pontil	7.00–9.00
on base: E J B	9 ⅛	Beverage	Brown	B.I.M.	2.00–2.50
NONE	8 ¾	Ale	Olive Green	B.I.M. Three-Piece Mold Whittle Marked Ground Pontil	7.00–9.00
NONE	9 ½	Wine	Olive Green	Free Blown Push Up	12.00–16.00

EMBOSSING	HEIGHT	TYPE	COLOR	HOW MADE	PRICE
Wm C. TRIPP TAUNTON MASS on back: THIS BOTTLE NOT TO BE SOLD	9 ¼	Beverage	Aqua	B.I.M.	2.50-3.50
VINCENT, HATHAWAY & CO. BOSTON GINGER ALE	8	Beverage	Aqua	B.I.M. Whittle Marked	3.50-4.50
LOUIS. A. GENT 211 & 213 EAST 94th ST N.Y. on back: TRADE MARK REGISTERED (mono LAG)	7 ½	Beverage	Aqua	B.I.M.	3.00-4.00
NONE	7 ½	Medicinal	Aqua	B.I.M. Whittle Marked	2.50-3.50
STANDARD BOTTLING CO. BOSTON MASS. (flag with 13 stars as shown)	7 ⅞	Beverage	Aqua	B.I.M. Whittle Marked	4.00-6.00

EMBOSSING	HEIGHT	TYPE	COLOR	HOW MADE	PRICE
F. H. BRADLEY & CO. BURLINGTON, N. J. THIS BOTTLE NOT TO BE SOLD	9 ⅜	Beverage	Deep Aqua	B.I.M.	2.50–3.50
REGISTERED G. F. HEWETT CO WORCESTER 1894 TRADE MARK G. F. H. CO (triangles on circle as shown)	8 ⅞	Beverage	Aqua	B.I.M.	2.50–3.50
REGISTERED DI STASIO & BRUNO 326 & 328 NORTH ST. BOSTON THIS BOTTLE NOT TO BE SOLD	9 ¼	Beverage	Clear	B.I.M.	2.00–3.00
THE BACHMANN BREWING CO CLIFTON ST'I. N. Y. THIS BOTTLE NOT TO BE SOLD	9	Beverage	Aqua	B.I.M. Whittle Marked	3.00–3.50
CROSBY AND BRADLEY 231 — 243 NUTFIELD LANE MANCHESTER N.H. REGISTERED	9 ¼	Beverage	S.C.A.	B.I.M.	3.00–3.50

EMBOSSING	HEIGHT	TYPE	COLOR	HOW MADE	PRICE
WASHINGTON SPRING SARATOGA N.Y.	8	Mineral Water	Emerald Green	B.I.M.	16.00-20.00
CONGRESS & EMPIRE SPRING CO SARATOGA, N. Y. (large C as shown) on back: CONGRESS WATER	7 ¾	Mineral Water	Emerald Green	B.I.M. Whittle Marked	14.00-18.00
CASWELL MACK & CO CHEMISTS NEW YORK & NEWPORT twin circles with words: LABOR OMNIA VINCIT	7 ⅜	Medicinal	Cobalt Blue	B.I.M. Whittle Marked	30.00-36.00
FAIRBANKS & BEARD HOWARD ST BOSTON (star as shown) on back: F & B	6 ¾	Mineral Water	Teal Green	B.I.M.	10.00-14.00
NONE	7 ⅛	Medicinal	Teal Green	B.I.M. Whittle Marked Glass Stopper Slug Plate Area	6.00-8.00

EMBOSSING	HEIGHT	TYPE	COLOR	HOW MADE	PRICE
NONE	9 ½	Soda or Mineral Water	Aqua	B.I.M.	2.00-3.00
KNIGHT AND McDONOUGH FIRST AND HENDERSON J.C. 1876	7 ⅝	Soda or Mineral Water	Aqua	B.I.M.	3.50-4.50
NONE on base: C.H.W.	7 ½	Soda or Mineral Water	Aqua	B.I.M. Whittle Marked	2.50-3.50
FRED HINCKEL NORMANSVILLE, N. Y. WEISS BEER TRADE MARK REGISTERED (initials FH as shown)	7 ⅜	Beer	Clear	B.I.M.	3.50-4.50
NONE	9 ⅛	Soda or Mineral Water	Aqua	B.I.M. Whittle Marked	3.00-3.50

EMBOSSING	HEIGHT	TYPE	COLOR	HOW MADE	PRICE
WARNER'S SAFE KIDNEY & LIVER CURE ROCHESTER, N. Y. (safe with 'trade mark' as shown)	9 ⅝	Medicinal	Amber	B.I.M.	10.00–14.00
ABSORBINE $2.00 PER BOTTLE M'F'G. BY W. F. YOUNG P.D.F. SPRINGFIELD, MASS. U.S.A.	7 ½	Medicinal (Liniment)	Amber	B.I.M. Strap-Sided	2.50–3.50
BOERICKE & RUNYON	8 ¾	Medicinal (Tablets)	Amber	B.I.M.	3.00–3.50
DOYLES HOP BITTERS 1872 (leaf as shown)	9 ⅜	Bitters	Amber	B.I.M.	40.00–48.00

EMBOSSING	HEIGHT	TYPE	COLOR	HOW MADE	PRICE
NONE	9 ⅝	Persian Saddle Trading Flask	Emerald Green	Free Blown Open Pontil	25.00-35.00
NONE	9 ½	Persian Saddle Trading Flask	Emerald Green	Free Blown Open Pontil	25.00-35.00

EMBOSSING	HEIGHT	TYPE	COLOR	HOW MADE	PRICE
NONE	13	Cathedral Pickle	Aqua	B.I.M.	30.00-40.00
NONE	13 ¼	Chemical	Brown	B.I.M.	2.50-3.50
NONE	13 ⅛	Cathedral Pickle	Aqua	B.I.M.	30.00-40.00

EMBOSSING	HEIGHT	TYPE	COLOR	HOW MADE	PRICE
NONE	11 ⅞	Demijohn	Olive Gold	Free Blown Rough Pontil	35.00–40.00
NONE	12 ¼	Demijohn	Gold	B.I.M.	10.00–12.00
NONE	11 ¾	Demijohn	Amber Gold	Three-Piece Mold	12.00–15.00

EMBOSSING	HEIGHT	TYPE	COLOR	HOW MADE	PRICE
ROBERT GIBSON MANCHESTER ENGLAND E. C. RICH NEW YORK U. S. AGENT	13	Tablets	Aqua	B.I.M.	3.00–4.00
NONE	10	Chemical	Aqua	B.I.M.	2.00–3.00
NONE	11 ¾	Medicinal	Aqua	B.I.M.	2.00–2.50

EMBOSSING	HEIGHT	TYPE	COLOR	HOW MADE	PRICE
PURE OLIVE OIL S.S.P.	11 ¾	Food	Clear	B.I.M.	3.50-4.50
PURE OLIVE OIL S.S.P.	9 ½	Food	Clear	B.I.M.	3.50-4.50
NONE	10 ⅞	Creme de Menthe	Clear	B.I.M.	2.50-3.50

EMBOSSING	HEIGHT	TYPE	COLOR	HOW MADE	PRICE
S. S. STAFFORD'S INKS MADE IN U.S.A. THIS BOTTLE CONTAINS ONE FULL QUART	9 ½	Master Ink	Cobalt Blue	B.I.M. Pouring Spout Lip	12.00–16.00
S.S. STAFFORD'S INKS MADE IN U.S.A.	7 ½	Master Ink	Cobalt Blue	B.I.M. Pouring Spout Lip	12.00–16.00
S.S. STAFFORD'S INKS MADE IN U.S.A	5 ⅞	Master Ink	Cobalt Blue	B.I.M. Pouring Spout Lip	12.00–16.00
STARKEY & PALEN PHILA COMPOUND OXYGEN	7 ¾	Medicinal	Cobalt Blue	B.I.M. Glass Stopper	7.00–9.00

EMBOSSING	HEIGHT	TYPE	COLOR	HOW MADE	PRICE
SMITHS WHITEROOT F & D	9 ½	Beer or Ale	Oatmeal	Pottery	4.00–6.00
NONE	8 ¼	Beer or Ale	Yellow Top Cream Base	Pottery	3.00–4.00
NELL CO MANCHESTER	10 ⅜	Whiskey or Rum	Brown Top to Lighter Base	Pottery	12.00–15.00

EMBOSSING	HEIGHT	TYPE	COLOR	HOW MADE	PRICE
NONE	8 ¼	Beer	Yellow and White Glaze	Pottery	3.00–4.00
B (circled)	3 ¼	Insulator	White	Ceramic	3.50–4.50
"AS YOU LIKE IT" TRADE MARK HORSE-RADISH.	3 ⅞	Food	Brown and White Glaze	Pottery	2.00–3.00
BLACKING BOTTLE	6 ½	Household	Cream Grey-Brown	Pottery	4.00–5.00

EMBOSSING	HEIGHT	TYPE	COLOR	HOW MADE	PRICE
ZEPP'S LUSTRAL FOR DANDRUFF T. NOONAN & CO. BOSTON	8 ⅜	Hair Conditioner	Clear	B.I.M.	2.50-3.50
NONE	8 ⅝	Cathedral Peppersauce	Aqua	B.I.M.	6.00-8.00
WONSITLER & Co DOYLESTOWN PA	7	Mineral Water	Deep Teal Green	B.I.M. Whittle Marked	15.00-18.00
JAMES KIDDER JR EAST BOSTON.	8 ½	Medicinal	Aqua	B.I.M. Whittle Marked	3.50-5.00
(paper label as shown) on sides: THE CUTICURA SYSTEM OF CURING CONSTITUTIONAL HUMORS POTTER DRUG & CHEMICAL CO BOSTON, MASS. U.S.A.	9 ¼	Medicinal	Aqua	B.I.M.	3.50-4.50

EMBOSSING	HEIGHT	TYPE	COLOR	HOW MADE	PRICE
NONE	10 ½	Medicinal (possibly castor oil)	Aqua	B.I.M.	2.50-3.00
NONE	9 ¼	Unknown	Aqua	B.I.M. Whittle Marked	3.50-4.50
FLORIDA WATER LAZELL, DALLEY & CO. NEW YORK	8 ½	Cosmetic	Aqua	B.I.M. Whittle Marked	3.50-4.50
SOLON PALMER'S FLORIDA WATER NEW YORK 7½ OZS. AVERAGE	8	Cosmetic	Aqua	B.I.M. Whittle Marked	3.50-4.50
GENUINE FLORIDA WATER PROF. GEO. J. BYRNE NEW YORK	8 ½	Cosmetic	Aqua	B.I.M. Whittle Marked	3.50-4.50
FLORIDA WATER MURRAY & LANMAN DRUGGISTS NEW - YORK	9	Cosmetic	Aqua	A.B.M.	2.00-2.50

EMBOSSING	HEIGHT	TYPE	COLOR	HOW MADE	PRICE
GRASSE LAUTIER OILS	8 ¼	Cosmetic	Clear	B.I.M. Glass Stopper	3.00-4.00
on base: DES. PAT. 81611	8 ⅞	Figural	Clear	A.B.M.	3.00-3.50
NONE	7 ¾	Unknown	Clear	Free Blown Pontil Marked	4.00-6.00
NONE	7 ⅜	Figural (Whiskey)	Blue	B.I.M.	10.00-14.00
THEO. RICKSECKER PERFUMER NEW YORK (initials as shown) mono on stopper: RICKER'S PERFUMES NEW YORK	6 ⅞	Cosmetic	Clear	B.I.M. Glass Stopper	3.50-5.00

EMBOSSING	HEIGHT	TYPE	COLOR	HOW MADE	PRICE
NONE (paper label as shown) on base: ESCOFFIER Ltd LONDON	8	Meat Sauce	Aqua	B.I.M. Metal Screw Cap	3.00-4.00
NONE (paper label as shown)	7 ⅞	Soy Sauce	Light Aqua	B.I.M.	3.00-4.00
THE J B WILLIAMS CO. GLASTONBURY, CT, U.S.A. on back: 6 FL. OZ. NET	6 ¾	Cosmetic	Clear	B.I.M.	2.00-2.50
NONE	7	Soyers Relish	Aqua	B.I.M.	4.00-5.00
IMPERIAL TOILET WATER VICTOR LEON PERFUMER PARIS (mono of crown as shown)	7 ½	Cosmetic	Light Grey Green	B.I.M.	3.00-4.00

EMBOSSING	HEIGHT	TYPE	COLOR	HOW MADE	PRICE
LEA & PERRINS WORCESTERSHIRE SAUCE	8 ½	Food	Light Green	B.I.M.	3.50–4.50
HOLBROOK & Co on two sides of neck: HOLBROOK	7 ½	Food (Sauce)	Blue Green	B.I.M.	3.50–4.50
ED. PINAUD PARIS (flowers as shown) on base: ED. PINAUD	6 ¾	Cosmetic	Clear	B.I.M.	2.50–3.50
Dr. WISTAR'S BALSAM OF WILD CHERRY PHILADa I. B.	6 ¼	Medicinal	Aqua	B.I.M. (Short Neck)	4.50–6.50
LARKIN CO. BUFFALO (initials as shown)	6 ⅝	Cosmetic	Aqua	B.I.M.	2.00–2.50
BURNETT BOSTON (initials as shown)	7 ⅞	Household	Light Green	B.I.M. Whittle Marked	2.00–3.00

EMBOSSING	HEIGHT	TYPE	COLOR	HOW MADE	PRICE
NONE (paper label as shown)	8	Embalming Fluid	Pink	A.B.M.	2.00-3.00
D. & M. Co. PROVIDENCE	8	Tablets	Clear	B.I.M.	2.00-3.00
NONE	6 ⅝	Cosmetic	Clear	B.I.M.	1.00-1.50
NONE (paper label as shown)	4 ¾	Medicinal	Clear	B.I.M. Glass Stopper	3.00-4.00
NONE (paper label as shown) on base: PAT'D MARCH 6th. 1894 ST. LOUIS MO.	6 ⅛	Hair Conditioner	Clear	B.I.M. Glass Stopper	3.00-4.00

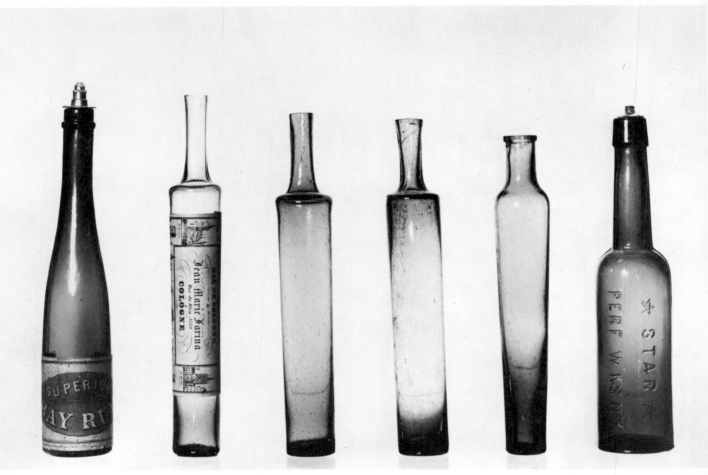

EMBOSSING	HEIGHT	TYPE	COLOR	HOW MADE	PRICE
NONE (paper label as shown)	8 ⅞	Cosmetic (After Shave Lotion)	Brown	B.I.M. Metal Spout Stopper	4.00–6.00
NONE (paper label as shown)	9 ¼	Cosmetic (Cologne)	Light Green	Free Blown Open Pontil	23.00–26.00
NONE	8 ¾	Cosmetic (Cologne)	Light Olive Green	Free Blown Open Pontil	22.00–25.00
NONE	8 ½	Wine Taster	Light Green	Free Blown Ground Pontil	18.00–22.00
NONE	8 ⅛	Cosmetic	Light Emerald Green	B.I.M.	5.00–7.00
STAR PERF' W'KS N.Y. (two stars as shown) (star on base)	8 ½	Cosmetic	Amber Brown	B.I.M. Metal Spout Stopper	4.00–6.00

EMBOSSING	HEIGHT	TYPE	COLOR	HOW MADE	PRICE
NONE	8 ⅛	Food (Capers)	Green	B.I.M.	7.00-9.00
NONE	6 ⅝	Food (Capers)	Green	B.I.M.	7.00-9.00
RUMFORD CHEMICAL WORKS (W with arch as shown)	5 ⅝	Medicinal	Teal Blue	B.I.M. Eight-Sided Panels	8.00-10.00
RUMFORD CHEMICAL WORKS (W with arch as shown)	5 ¾	Medicinal	Teal Blue	B.I.M. Eight-Sided Panel	8.00-10.00
NOONAN'S HAIR PETROLE 8 FL. OZS. CAP. REG. U.S. PAT. OFF. T. NOONAN & SONS CO. BOSTON MASS. MADE IN U.S.A.	6 ⅜	Hair Conditioner	Blue	A.B.M. Metal Stopper	2.00-3.00
NONE	7	Taper Gin	Green	B.I.M.	10.00-15.00

EMBOSSING	HEIGHT	TYPE	COLOR	HOW MADE	PRICE
FOOD EXTRACTS HEALTH FOOD CO. NEW YORK.	5 ⅝	Food	Aqua	B.I.M.	2.00-2.50
MELLIN'S INFANT'S FOOD DOLIBER, GOODALE & CO BOSTON	5 ½	Food	Aqua	B.I.M.	2.50-3.50
MELLIN'S INFANT'S FOOD DOLIBER — GOODALE CO BOSTON	5 ⅛	Food	Aqua	B.I.M.	2.50-3.50
NONE	5 ⅛	Food	Aqua	B.I.M.	1.00-1.50
NONE	6 ¼	Master Ink	Aqua	B.I.M.	5.00-7.00
H. H. HAY & SON — LF — on base: L. F. ATWOOD	6 ⅝	Medicinal	Aqua	B.I.M.	2.00-3.00

EMBOSSING	HEIGHT	TYPE	COLOR	HOW MADE	PRICE
NONE	7 ¼	Medicinal	Aqua	B.I.M. Whittle Marked	2.50-3.50
NONE (paper label as shown)	6 ⅝	Food (Pickles)	Aqua	B.I.M.	2.00-3.00
NONE	6 ⅛	Food	Aqua	B.I.M.	1.00-1.50
NONE	6 ⅜	Medicinal	Aqua	B.I.M.	1.50-2.00
NONE	7 ½	Food (Pickles)	Aqua	B.I.M.	2.00-2.50

EMBOSSING	HEIGHT	TYPE	COLOR	HOW MADE	PRICE
NONE	7 ⅝	Pickle or Preserve	Clear	B.I.M.	1.00–1.50
NONE	7	Pickle or Preserve	S.C.A.	B.I.M.	1.50–2.00
NONE	6	Condiment	S.C.A.	B.I.M.	1.50–2.00
NONE	7 ⅛	Food	Clear	B.I.M.	2.00–2.50
NONE	9 ½	Pickle or Preserve	S.C.A.	B.I.M.	3.00–4.00

EMBOSSING	HEIGHT	TYPE	COLOR	HOW MADE	PRICE
on base: S & P PAT. APP. FOR	8 ⅛	Food (Pepper Sauce)	Emerald Green	B.I.M.	10.00-12.00
NONE	8 ⅛	Food (Pepper Sauce)	Aqua	B.I.M.	6.00-8.00
CURTICE BROTHERS CO. PRESERVERS ROCHESTER, N. Y.	8	Food (Ketchup)	Clear	B.I.M.	2.00-2.50
on base: LINONINE DANBURY CONN.	6 ⅝	Medicinal	Aqua	B.I.M.	1.50-2.00
NONE	7 ½	Food (Olive Oil)	Light Green	B.I.M.	3.50-4.50
NONE	7 ¼	Wine	Light Green	Turn Mold Push Up	2.50-3.50

EMBOSSING	HEIGHT	TYPE	COLOR	HOW MADE	PRICE
THE HERO on base: PATd NOV 26 1867.	7 ⅛	Pickle or Preserve	Aqua	B.I.M. Ground Top	4.00-6.00
NONE	8 ⅛	Preserve	Aqua	B.I.M.	3.00-3.50
NONE	6 ¼	Battery Jar	Aqua	B.I.M. Ground Top Whittle Marked	3.00-3.50

EMBOSSING	HEIGHT	TYPE	COLOR	HOW MADE	PRICE
MASON'S IMPROVED (maltese cross as shown) on base: PAT NOV 26 67	9 ¼	Preserves	Aqua	B.I.M. Ground Top	5.00-6.00
DAISY	7 ½	Preserves	S.C.A.	A.B.M.	2.50-3.00
MASON'S PATENT NOV 30th 1858 on base: P. B. 2	5 ⅝	Preserves	Clear	B.I.M. Ground Top Whittle Marked	4.50-6.00
ROYAL TRADE MARK FULL MEASURE REGISTERED QUART (crown as shown) on base: A. G. SMALLEY & CO. BOSTON & NEW YORK PATENTED APRIL 7th 1896	7 ½	Preserves	Amber	B.I.M. Ground Top	10.00-14.00

EMBOSSING	HEIGHT	TYPE	COLOR	HOW MADE	PRICE
MASON'S PATENT NOV 30th 1858 (mono as shown)	7 ⅛	Preserves	Aqua	B.I.M. Ground Top Whittle Marked	5.00–6.00
MASON'S PATENT NOV 30th 1858 (mono on reverse)	6 ¾	Preserves	Aqua	B.I.M. Ground Top	3.00–3.50
MASON'S PATENT NOV. 30th 1858 (maltese cross as shown) on base: PAT NOV 26 67	7 ⅛	Preserves	Aqua	B.I.M. Ground Top	5.00–6.00
MASON'S IMPROVED (mono as shown)	6 ⅞	Preserves	Aqua	B.I.M. Ground Top Whittle Marked	5.00–6.00

EMBOSSING	HEIGHT	TYPE	COLOR	HOW MADE	PRICE
R.E.T. & Bros. CO. INC. PHILA, PA. U.S.A. OUR-SEAL on base: R.E. TONGUE & BROS. CO. INC: PHILA, PA. OUR SEAL PATENTED JAN 5 1904	7	Preserves	Clear	A.B.M.	1.50-2.00
ELECTRIC FRUIT JAR (mono as shown) on base: PAT APP FOR	7 ⅛	Preserves	Aqua	B.I.M. Ground Top Whittle Marked	6.00-8.00
TRADE MARK LIGHTNING REGISTERED U.S. PATENT OFFICE on base: PUTNAM 19	5 ⅝	Preserves	Aqua	A.B.M.	2.00-2.50
DOUBLE SAFETY on base: SMALLEY KIVLAN & ONTHANK BOSTON, MASS. on collar: TIGHT	7 ½	Preserves	Clear	A.B.M.	1.50-2.00

EMBOSSING	HEIGHT	TYPE	COLOR	HOW MADE	PRICE
on back: Dr CUMMING'S VEGETINE (paper label as shown)	9 ¾	Medicinal	Aqua	B.I.M.	3.50-5.00
NONE	9	Medicinal	Aqual	Three-Piece Mold	2.50-3.00
NONE	9 ½	Beverage	Aqua	B.I.M. Whittle Marked	3.00-3.50
NONE	10 ⅛	Olive Oil	Aqua	Turn Mold	3.50-4.50

EMBOSSING	HEIGHT	TYPE	COLOR	HOW MADE	PRICE
NONE	8 ¾	Chemical	Clear	Three-Piece Mold Glass Stopper	2.50-3.50
NONE (paper label as shown)	8 ⅞	Household	Aqua	B.I.M.	2.00-3.00
NONE	8 ½	Medicinal (Tablets)	Aqua	B.I.M.	1.50-2.50
NONE	9 ½	Medicinal	Aqua	Free Blown Open Pontil	7.00-9.00

EMBOSSING	HEIGHT	TYPE	COLOR	HOW MADE	PRICE
J. R. NICHOLS & CO. CHEMISTS BOSTON	10 ⅛	Medicinal	Aqua	B.I.M.	3.50-4.50
NONE (paper label as shown)	8 ⅞	Bitters	Aqua	B.I.M.	4.00-6.00
SILVER PINE HEALING OIL INTERNATIONAL FOOD CO. MINNEAPOLIS, MINN.	8 ⅛	Medicinal	Aqua	B.I.M.	3.00-4.00
RUSH'S SARSAPARILLA AND IRON A. H. FLANDER'S MD NEW YORK	8 ⅞	Medicinal	Aqua	B.I.M.	8.00-12.00
PHILLIPS' PALATABLE COD LIVER OIL WITH PHOSPO-NUTRITINE	9 ⅝	Medicinal	Blue	B.I.M.	2.50-3.50

EMBOSSING	HEIGHT	TYPE	COLOR	HOW MADE	PRICE
Dr PIERCE'S GOLDEN MEDICAL DISCOVERY R.V. PIERCE, M. D. BUFFALO, N. Y.	8 ⅝	Medicinal	Aqua	B.I.M.	3.00-4.00
Dr TOBIAS VENETIAN HORSE LINIMENT NEW YORK	8 ⅛	Medicinal	Aqua	B.I.M. Whittle Marked	3.50-4.50
WHEELER'S TISSUE PHOSPHATES	8 ⅝	Medicinal	Aqua	B.I.M.	3.00-4.00
ELMER'S GREAT FRENCH REMEDY PROVIDENCE, R.I. U.S.A. GEO. W. ELMER & CO. MANUFACTURERS	8 ⅛	Medicinal	Aqua	B.I.M.	3.00-4.00
Dr HARTSHORN & SONS BOSTON	8 ⅜	Medicinal	Aqua	B.I.M.	3.00-4.00

EMBOSSING	HEIGHT	TYPE	COLOR	HOW MADE	PRICE
WEST END WINE & SPIRITS CO 15 - 19 LEVERETT ST. BOSTON, MASS.	8 ¼	Whiskey	Aqua	B.I.M.	2.50-3.50
THE PURDUE FREDERICK CO NEW YORK (initials as shown)	7 ¾	Medicinal	Clear	B.I.M. Strap-Sided	2.50-3.50
FLORIDA WATER	9	Cosmetic	Aqua	B.I.M.	3.00-4.00
HOLLINGS - SMITH CO. MANUFACTURING CHEMISTS ORANGEBURG, NEW YORK, U.S.A.	7 ⅞	Medicinal (Pills)	Clear	B.I.M.	2.50-3.50
THE ZEMMER CO. MANUFACTURING CHEMISTS PITTSBURG, PA.	9 ¼	Medicinal (Pills)	Clear	B.I.M.	2.50-3.50

EMBOSSING	HEIGHT	TYPE	COLOR	HOW MADE	PRICE
GUARANTEED FULL PINT. P. DEMPSEY & CO. BOSTON, MASS. REGISTERED.	8 ¾	Whiskey	Clear	B.I.M.	2.00-3.00
SCOTT'S EMULSION COD LIVER OIL WITH LIME & SODA (man with codfish on base)	7 ⅝	Medicinal	Aqua	B.I.M.	2.50-3.50
Drs F. E. & J. A. GREENE NEW YORK & BOSTON	7 ¼	Medicinal	Light Green	B.I.M.	2.50-3.50
DR. KING'S NEW DISCOVERY FOR CONSUMPTION H. E. BUCKLEN & CO. CHICAGO, ILL.	8	Medicinal	Aqua	B.I.M.	2.50-3.50
GUARANTEED FULL PINT D. J. KEEFE & CO. 109 & 111 DARTMOUTH ST. BOSTON, MASS.	9	Whiskey	Clear	B.I.M.	2.00-3.00

EMBOSSING	HEIGHT	TYPE	COLOR	HOW MADE	PRICE
PHILLIP'S EMULSION COD LIVER OIL NEW YORK	7 ½	Medicinal	Brown Amber	B.I.M.	3.50-4.50
BROWN MANUFACTURING CO GREENEVILLE, TENN NEW YORK, N. Y.	7 ½	Medicinal	Amber	B.I.M.	3.00-4.00
MY WIFE'S SALAD DRESSING	7 ¾	Food	Gold	B.I.M.	5.00-7.00
CELERY MEDICINE CO. KALAMAZOO, MICH.	9	Medicinal	Brown Amber	B.I.M.	4.50-6.50
NONE	8 ⅞	Chemical	Brown Amber	B.I.M.	2.00-3.00

EMBOSSING	HEIGHT	TYPE	COLOR	HOW MADE	PRICE
LYDIA E PINKHAM'S VEGETABLE COMPOUND	8 ¾	Medicinal	Aqua	B.I.M.	2.50-3.50
THE GREAT DR. KILMER'S SWAMP-ROOT KIDNEY LIVER & BLADDER CURE SPECIFIC DR. KILMER & CO. BINGHAMTON, N. Y.	8 ⅜	Medicinal	Clear	B.I.M.	5.00-7.00
LYDIA E. PINKHAM'S VEGETABLE COMPOUND	8 ¼	Medicinal	Aqua	B.I.M.	2.50-3.50
ALLEN'S SARSAPARILLA	8 ⅜	Medicinal	Aqua	B.I.M.	10.00-15.00

EMBOSSING	HEIGHT	TYPE	COLOR	HOW MADE	PRICE
SCOTT'S EMULSION COD LIVER OIL WITH LIME & SODA	9 ⅛	Medicinal	Aqua	B.I.M.	2.00-3.00
NONE	8 ¾	Medicinal	Aqua	B.I.M.	1.00-1.50
Dr KENNEDY'S MEDICAL DISCOVERY ROXBURY MASS	8 ⅞	Medicinal	Aqua	B.I.M.	2.50-4.00
AYER'S SARSAPARILLA LOWELL MASS, U.S.A.	8 ½	Medicinal	Aqua	A.B.M.	3.50-5.00
AYER'S SARSAPARILLA COMPOUND EXT.	8 ½	Medicinal	Aqua	B.I.M.	2.50-4.50

EMBOSSING	HEIGHT	TYPE	COLOR	HOW MADE	PRICE
HAAS PHARMACY	8 ¼	Medicinal	Clear	B.I.M.	2.50-3.00
BONNIE BROS. LOUISVILLE, KY. (emblem with 'BONNIE' as shown)	8 ½	Whiskey	Clear	B.I.M.	3.00-4.00
CREOMULSION FOR COUGHS DUE TO COLDS	8 ⅜	Medicinal	Clear	A.B.M.	1.00-1.50
ESTABLISHED 1851 W. H. JONES & CO IMPORTERS HANOVER AND BLACKSTONE STS. BOSTON, MASS. (mono trade mark as shown)	8 ½	Whiskey	Clear	B.I.M.	2.00-2.50
on opposite side panels: BLOOD WINE THE LOUIS DAUDELIN CO.	8 ⅝	Medicinal	Clear	B.I.M.	2.50-3.00

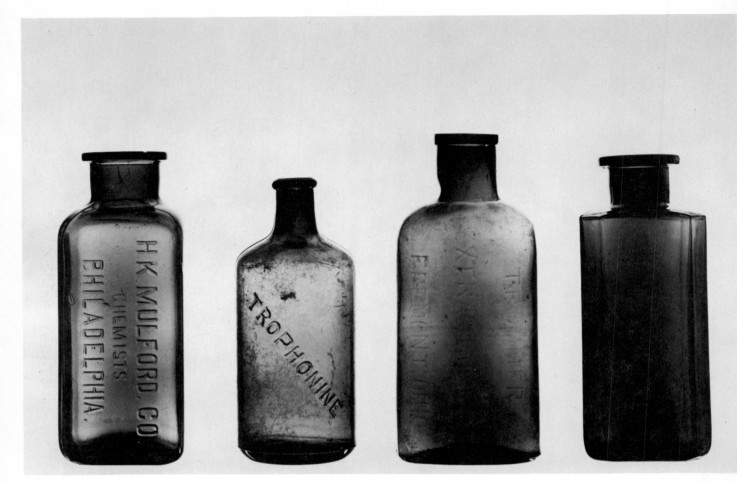

EMBOSSING	HEIGHT	TYPE	COLOR	HOW MADE	PRICE
H. K. MULFORD, CO. CHEMISTS PHILADELPHIA.	7 ⅞	Medicinal	Amber	B.I.M.	3.50-4.50
TROPHONINE on base: REED & CARNICK N.Y.	7 ¼	Medicinal	Amber	B.I.M.	2.50-3.50
TROMMER EXTRACT OF MALT CO FREMONT OHIO	8 ¼	Malt Extract	Brown	B.I.M.	4.00-4.50
NONE	7 ⅜	Medicinal (Tablets)	Brown	B.I.M.	2.00-3.00

EMBOSSING	HEIGHT	TYPE	COLOR	HOW MADE	PRICE
SLOAN'S LINIMENT FOR MAN OR BEAST DR. EARL S. SLOAN, INC. BOSTON, U.S.A. LONDON, ENG.	3 ⅜	Medicinal	Clear	B.I.M.	2.50-3.50
SCHENCK'S SEAWEED TONIC	9	Medicinal	Aqua	B.I.M.	5.00-6.50
THE TWITCHELL CHAMPLIN CO'S FLAVORING EXTRACTS PORTLAND BOSTON	7 ⅝	Food	Aqua	B.I.M. Whittle Marked	2.50-3.50
THE ALMYR SYSTEM OF TREATMENT FOR DISEASES OF THE SKIN AND BLOOD ALMYR BLOOD CLEANSER	8 ⅛	Medicinal	Aqua	B.I.M.	3.00-4.00
ONE PINT T. NOONAN & SONS CO. BOSTON, MASS.	8 ½	Medicinal	S.C.A.	B.I.M.	3.00-4.00

EMBOSSING	HEIGHT	TYPE	COLOR	HOW MADE	PRICE
NONE (paper label as shown)	7	Medicinal	Amber Brown	B.I.M.	2.50–3.50
HAIR BALSAM PARKER'S NEW YORK	7 ½	Hair Conditioner	Amber Brown	B.I.M.	3.50–4.50
WORLDS HAIR RESTORER MRS. S.A. ALLEN'S NEW YORK	7 ½	Hair Conditioner	Amber	B.I.M.	3.50–4.50
on opposite side panels: LUBYS FOR THE HAIR	7 ⅝	Hair Conditioner	Amber Brown	B.I.M.	3.00–4.00
RAWLEIGH'S	8 ⅜	Extract	Amber Brown	A.B.M.	1.00–2.00

EMBOSSING	HEIGHT	TYPE	COLOR	HOW MADE	PRICE
(paper label as shown) on back: Dr PIERCE'S FAVORITE MEDICAL DISCOVERY R. V. PIERCE, M.D. BUFFALO, N.Y.	8	Medicinal	Aqua	B.I.M.	3.50-4.50
Dr PIERCE'S FAVORITE PRESCRIPTION R.V. PIERCE, M. D. BUFFALO, N. Y.	8	Medicinal	Aqua	B.I.M.	3.00-4.00
Dr PIERCE'S FAVORITE PRESCRIPTION R. V. PIERCE, M.D. BUFFALO, N. Y.	8	Medicinal	Green	A.B.M.	2.00-3.00
BLANCARD	7	Medicinal	Light Green	B.I.M.	3.50-4.50
NATHAN WOOD & SON, PROPRIETORS, PORTLAND, MAINE. ATWELL'S HEALTH RESTORER	7 ¼	Medicinal	Aqua	B.I.M.	2.00-3.00

EMBOSSING	HEIGHT	TYPE	COLOR	HOW MADE	PRICE
DR MCARTHUR MAKER CHEMICALLY PURE SYRUP OF HYPOPHOSPHITES	6 ½	Medicinal	Clear	B.I.M.	2.00-2.50
ACID LINE MANUFACTURED BY BADGER FIRE EXTINGUISHER COMPANY BOSTON, MASS. U.S.A.	6	Chemical	Clear	B.I.M.	1.50-2.50

SODIUM PHOSPHATE
$NA^2 HPO^4$
on base: PAT. MAR 25 1879
     WHITALL TATUM & CO
     PHILA U.S.A. NEW YORK
	5 ½	Chemical	Clear	B.I.M.	2.00-3.00

NONE (mono as shown)	5 ½	Cosmetic	S.C.A.	B.I.M. Glass Stopper	3.50-4.50
VANTINES EASTERN PERFUMES NEW YORK YOKOHAMA CONSTANTINOPLE HONG KONG BOMBAY SINGAPORE (monos as shown)	7 ⅛	Cosmetic	Clear	B.I.M.	2.50-3.50
ED. PINAUD PARIS (mono as shown)	6 ⅞	Cosmetic	Clear	B.I.M.	2.50-3.50

EMBOSSING	HEIGHT	TYPE	COLOR	HOW MADE	PRICE
SWAIM'S PANACEA TRADE MARK ESTABLISHED 1820 ST. LOUIS, MO.	8 ⅛	Medicinal	Clear	B.I.M.	4.00–5.00
COLGATE & CO NEW YORK (design as shown)	6 ¼	Cosmetic	Clear	B.I.M.	3.50–4.50
CHAMPION SPOUTING SPRING CO SARATOGA SPRINGS N. Y. on back: C S S	7 ½	Mineral Water	Aqua	B.I.M. Whittle Marked	8.00–10.00
NONE	6 ¾	Cordial	Clear	Turn Mold	3.00–4.00

EMBOSSING	HEIGHT	TYPE	COLOR	HOW MADE	PRICE
NONE	9 ⅛	Medicinal	Clear	B.I.M. Glass Stopper Open Pontil	7.00-10.00
NONE	6⅝	Medicinal	Clear	B.I.M. Glass Stopper Open Pontil	7.00-10.00
NONE	6 ½	Medicinal	Clear	B.I.M. Glass Stopper Open Pontil	7.00-10.00
NONE	6 ¼	Medicinal	Clear	B.I.M. Glass Stopper Open Pontil	7.00-10.00

EMBOSSING	HEIGHT	TYPE	COLOR	HOW MADE	PRICE
Dr KENNEDY'S MEDICAL DISCOVERY ROXBURY MASS	8 ⅝	Medicinal	Aqua	B.I.M.	3.50-4.50
on back: GUARANTEED FULL PINT (paper label as shown)	8 ⅝	Whiskey	Clear	B.I.M.	2.50-3.50
OXOLO	8	Unknown	Aqua	B.I.M. Strap-Sided	2.50-3.00
THE GREAT DR. KILMER'S SWAMP-ROOT KIDNEY LIVER & BLADDER REMEDY BINGHAMTON, N. Y.	8 ⅛	Medicinal	Aqua	B.I.M.	5.00-6.00

EMBOSSING	HEIGHT	TYPE	COLOR	HOW MADE	PRICE
NONE	7 ⅜	Medicinal	Cobalt Blue	B.I.M.	3.50-4.50
AYER'S HAIR VIGOR	6 ¼	Medicinal	Peacock Blue	B.I.M.	12.00-16.00
NONE	5 ⅞	Medicinal	Cobalt Blue	B.I.M.	3.00-3.50
LIQUOZONE MANUFACTURED ONLY BY THE LIQUOZONE CO. CHICAGO, U.S.A.	5 ½	Medicinal	Amber Brown	B.I.M.	2.50-3.50
NONE	6 ⅛	Medicinal	Amber Brown	B.I.M. Four-Piece Mold Whittle Marked	2.50-3.50
NONE	6 ⅝	Taper Gin	Light Olive Green	B.I.M.	8.00-10.00

EMBOSSING	HEIGHT	TYPE	COLOR	HOW MADE	PRICE
FATHER JOHN'S MEDICINE LOWELL, MASS.	7 ¼	Medicinal	Brown Amber	B.I.M.	4.00-5.00
NONE (paper label as shown)	4 ⅞	Medicinal	Amber	B.I.M.	2.50-3.50
NONE (paper label as shown)	4 ½	Medicinal	Amber	B.I.M.	2.50-3.50
on opposite sides: MAGGI	5 ¾	Food (Meat Sauce)	Red Amber	B.I.M.	4.50-5.00
on all four sides: MAGGI (number 2 and mono as shown)	6 ¼	Food (Meat Sauce)	Amber	B.I.M.	4.00-5.00
NONE	7 ⅜	Medicinal	Light Olive Gold	B.I.M. Strap-Sided	3.00-4.00

EMBOSSING	HEIGHT	TYPE	COLOR	HOW MADE	PRICE
CARBONOL "NECESSARY AS SOAP"	5 ⅜	Household	Clear	B.I.M.	1.50-2.00
PAUL WESTPHAL AUXILIATOR FOR THE HAIR NEW YORK	6 ⅝	Cosmetic	Clear	B.I.M.	2.00-3.00
NONE	7 ⅝	Medicinal	Blue	B.I.M.	3.00-4.50
NONE on base: WYETH 209	7 ½	Medicinal	Amber	B.I.M.	2.50-3.50
ORCUTT'S SURE RHEUMATIC CURE	6 ⅛	Medicinal	Cobalt Blue	B.I.M.	4.50-5.50
NONE	5 ½	Chemical	Amber	B.I.M.	2.00-2.50

EMBOSSING	HEIGHT	TYPE	COLOR	HOW MADE	PRICE
S. O. RICHARDSON'S BITTERS SOUTH READING MASS.	6 ⅞	Bitters	Aqua	B.I.M. Whittle Marked	22.00–28.00
SCHENCK'S PULMONIC SYRUP PHILADa	7	Medicinal	Aqua	B.I.M.	4.00–6.00
Dr WISTAR'S BALSAM OF WILD CHERRY PHILADa	6 ¼	Medicinal	Aqua	B.I.M.	4.00–6.00
Dr. WISTAR'S BALSAM OF WILD CHERRY PHILADa	6 ⅜	Medicinal	Aqua	B.I.M.	4.00–6.00
NONE	7 ⅞	Medicinal	Aqua	B.I.M. Open Pontil Whittle Marked	9.00–12.00

EMBOSSING	HEIGHT	TYPE	COLOR	HOW MADE	PRICE
CHAMBERLAIN'S COUGH REMEDY CHAMBERLAIN MED. CO DES MOINES, IOWA	7	Medicinal	Aqua	B.I.M.	2.50-3.00
DR. W. B. CALDWELL'S MONTICELLO, ILLINOIS	7	Medicinal	Aqua	A.B.M.	1.00-1.50
NONE (paper label as shown)	6 ½	Cosmetic (After Shave Lotion)	Clear	B.I.M.	1.50-2.00
E. HARTSHORN & SONS BOSTON ESTABLISHED 1860 (initials as shown)	6 ¼	Medicinal	Aqua	B.I.M.	2.00-2.50
THE BARKER MOORE & MEIN MEDICINE COMPANY PHILADELPHIA	6 ¼	Medicinal	Aqua	B.I.M.	2.00-2.50
NONE	6 ⅝	Medicinal	Aqua	B.I.M.	1.50-2.00

EMBOSSING	HEIGHT	TYPE	COLOR	HOW MADE	PRICE
ATWOOD'S JAUNDICE BITTERS MOSES ATWOOD GEORGETOWN MASS (paper label as shown)	6	Bitters	Aqua	B.I.M.	5.00–7.00
ATWOOD'S JAUNDICE BITTERS MOSES ATWOOD GEORGETOWN, MASS.	6	Bitters	Aqua	B.I.M.	4.00–6.00
POND'S EXTRACT on base: 1846 (paper label as shown)	5 ⅜	Medicinal	Aqua	B.I.M.	3.00–4.00
ARNICA & OIL LINIMENT	6 ⅝	Medicinal	Light Green	B.I.M.	2.50–3.50
COURTENAY & Co WORCESTERSHIRE SAUCE	6 ⅞	Food	Aqua	B.I.M. Whittle Marked	2.50–3.00
KEASBEY & MATTISON PHILADELPHIA	6 ¼	Medicinal	Light Blue	B.I.M.	2.50–3.50
JOHNSON'S AMERICAN ANODYNE LINIMENT	6 ¼	Medicinal	Aqua	B.I.M.	2.50–3.50

EMBOSSING	HEIGHT	TYPE	COLOR	HOW MADE	PRICE
NONE (paper label as shown)	6 ⅞	Medicinal (Chloroform)	Brown	Three-Piece Mold	2.00-3.00
on opposite sides: MEDICINAL SOLUTION OF PYROZONE 3% $H_2 O_2$ McKESSON & ROBBINS NEW YORK (paper label as shown)	5 ⅛	Medicinal	Amber	B.I.M. Glass Stopper	3.00-3.50
on back: OTIS CLAPP & SON INCORPORATED (paper label as shown)	6	Medicinal	Amber	B.I.M.	2.50-3.00
6 OZ. FARR'S GRAY HAIR RESTORER BOSTON MASS.	5 ½	Hair Conditioner	Amber Brown	A.B.M.	1.50-2.50
NONE	6	Medicinal	Amber	B.I.M.	1.50-2.00
THE OAKLAND CHEMICAL COMP'Y (mono $H_2 O_2$ as shown)	6	Household	Amber	B.I.M.	2.00-2.50

EMBOSSING	HEIGHT	TYPE	COLOR	HOW MADE	PRICE
CALIFORNIA FIG SYRUP CO. SAN FRANCISCO, CAL. on each side panel: SYRUP OF FIGS	7	Laxative	Clear	B.I.M.	2.00-2.50
NONE	7	Medicinal	Clear	B.I.M.	1.00-1.50
EASTMAN ROCHESTER, N.Y.	6 ¼	Chemical	Clear	B.I.M.	2.00-2.50
DILLON'S PAIN EASE YPSILANTI, MICH. (paper label as shown)	6 ¾	Medicinal	Clear	B.I.M.	2.50-3.00
LARKIN CO. BUFFALO	7	Cosmetic	Clear	B.I.M.	1.50-2.00
GUARANTEED FULL ½ PINT CHAS G. GOVE CO. 168 CANAL ST. BOSTON, MASS.	7 ¼	Liquor	Clear	B.I.M.	2.00-2.50

EMBOSSING	HEIGHT	TYPE	COLOR	HOW MADE	PRICE
JOHN WYETH & BRO. on base: PAT APPD. FOR on cap: numbers 1-12 and THIS CUP HOLDS A DOSE	5 ⅞	Medicinal	Cobalt Blue	B.I.M.	8.00-10.00
JOHN WYETH & BRO. on base: PAT. MAY 16th 1899 on cap: numbers 1-12 and THIS CUP HOLDS A DOSE	6 ½	Medicinal	Cobalt Blue	A.B.M.	7.00-9.00
THE MALTINE MFG CO NEW YORK	6 ⅜	Medicinal	Amber	B.I.M.	3.00-4.00
A. L. MURDOCK LIQUID FOOD BOSTON 12½ PER CENT SOLUBLE ALBUMEN TRADE MARK	5 ¾	Medicinal	Amber Brown	B.I.M.	3.50-4.50
GRANULAR-CITRATE OF.MAGNESIA	6	Medicinal	Dark Blue	B.I.M.	4.00-6.00
NONE	5 ⅞	Medicinal	Cobalt Blue	B.I.M.	3.00-3.50

EMBOSSING	HEIGHT	TYPE	COLOR	HOW MADE	PRICE
NONE	6 ½	Medicinal	Aqua	B.I.M.	1.50-2.00
NONE	6 ½	Liquor	Aqua	B.I.M.	1.50-2.00
BURNETT'S COCOAINE BURNETT BOSTON	6	Medicinal	Aqua	B.I.M.	3.50-4.50
RAWLEIGH'S TRADE MARK W. T. RAWLEIGH CO. FREEPORT, ILL.	6 ¼	Extract	Aqua	A.B.M.	1.00-1.50
DR. S. A. TUTTLE BOSTON MASS	6 ⅝	Medicinal	Aqua	B.I.M.	2.00-2.50
KEMP'S BALSAM FOR THROAT AND LUNGS O. F. WOODWARD LEROY, N.Y.	6 ½	Medicinal	Aqua	B.I.M.	2.50-3.00

EMBOSSING	HEIGHT	TYPE	COLOR	HOW MADE	PRICE
C. H. MARTIN CO. APOTHECARIES CONCORD, N.H.	6 ⅝	Medicinal	Clear	B.I.M.	1.50-2.00
NONE	5	Cosmetic	Clear	B.I.M. Three-Piece Mold Glass Stopper	1.50-2.50
WHITTEMORE BOSTON on back: FRENCH GLOSS	4 ¾	Household	Aqua	B.I.M.	1.50-2.00
KDC FOR DYSPEPSIA	4 ⅜	Medicinal	Aqua	B.I.M.	2.00-2.50
THE TOILETINE CO. REG. U.S. TOILETINE PAT. OFF. GREENFIELD, MASS.	4 ⅞	Cosmetic	Clear	B.I.M.	1.50-2.00
H. H. RICKER & Co. PORTLAND ME.	5 ⅜	Medicinal	Aqua	B.I.M.	1.50-2.00
MASCARO TONIQUE FOR THE HAIR MARTHA MATILDA HARPER ROCHESTER. N.Y. U.S.A. TRADE MARK (mono as shown)	6 ⅜	Hair Conditioner	Clear	B.I.M.	2.50-3.00

EMBOSSING	HEIGHT	TYPE	COLOR	HOW MADE	PRICE
PETTS BOSTON	6 ¼	Whiskey	Clear	B.I.M.	2.50–3.50
WARRANTED FLASK	5 ¼	Whiskey	Clear	B.I.M.	3.00–3.50
HAMILTON'S OLD ENGLISH BLACK OIL	4 ⅝	Household	S.C.A.	B.I.M. Seven-Sided Panels	3.00–4.00
NONE	5	Unknown	Aqua	Free Blown Open Pontil	7.00–9.00
SOLON PALMER'S FLORIDA WATER NEW YORK	6 ¼	Cosmetic	Aqua	B.I.M.	2.50–3.00
ST JAKOB'S OEL A. VOGELER & CO BALTIMORE MD	6 ⅜	Medicinal	Aqua	B.I.M. Whittle Marked	2.50–3.50

EMBOSSING	HEIGHT	TYPE	COLOR	HOW MADE	PRICE
NONE (paper label as shown)	6 ⅞	Medicinal	Aqua	B.I.M.	3.00-3.50
DR TOBIAS NEW YORK VENETIAN LINIMENT	6 ⅜	Medicinal	Aqua	B.I.M. Whittle Marked Ground Pontil	5.00-7.00
DR TOBIAS NEW YORK VENETIAN LINIMENT	5 ¾	Medicinal	Deep Aqua	B.I.M. Open Pontil	12.00-15.00
DR TOBIAS NEW YORK VENETIAN LINIMENT	5 ¾	Medicinal	Aqua	B.I.M. Open Pontil Whittle Marked	12.00-16.00
NONE	5	Medicinal	Aqua	Free Blown Open Pontil	7.00-10.00
MAGIC HAIR INVIGORATOR PROFESSOR MOTTs PRICE 50 CENTS HENRY & CO. BURLINGTON VT.	6 ⅜	Medicinal	Aqua	B.I.M. Whittle Marked Ground Pontil	5.00-7.00

EMBOSSING	HEIGHT	TYPE	COLOR	HOW MADE	PRICE
NONE	5 ¾	Medicinal (Tablets)	Amber Brown	B.I.M.	2.00-2.50
NONE (paper label as shown)	5 ¼	Medicinal	Amber Brown	B.I.M.	2.00-2.50
PHOSPHO-CAFFEIN COMP. ARLINGTON CHEMICAL CO YONKERS, N.Y.	4 ⅞	Medicinal	Amber Brown	B.I.M.	2.00-2.50
THE DUFFY MALT WHISKEY COMPANY ROCHESTER, N.Y. U.S.A. (embossed mono as shown) on base: PATd AUG. 24 1886	6	Whiskey Sampler	Amber	B.I.M.	7.00-9.00
NONE	5 ⅝	Cosmetic (Toilet Water)	Clear	B.I.M.	2.00-5.00
NONE	5 ⅜	Cosmetic (Toilet Water)	Dark Teal Green	B.I.M.	10.00-15.00
THE CORPORATION OF HEGEMAN & CO PERFUMERS 200 BROADWAY NEW YORK	5 ⅜	Cosmetic	Dark Teal Green	B.I.M. Glass Stopper	10.00-16.00

EMBOSSING	HEIGHT	TYPE	COLOR	HOW MADE	PRICE
GEO R EMERSON WEST SOMERVILLE	5 ⅜	Unknown	Aqua	B.I.M.	2.50-3.00
WHITTEMORE BOSTON	5	Household	Aqua	B.I.M.	1.50-2.50
ELLIMAN'S EMBROCATION	5 ½	Medicinal	Aqua	B.I.M.	2.50-3.50
HAND MED. CO. PHILADELPHIA	5 ¼	Medicinal	Aqua	B.I.M.	1.50-2.00
PHILLIPS' MILK OF MAGNESIA REG. IN U.S. PAT. OFFICE AUG. 21, 1906 (mono with trade mark as shown)	4 ⅞	Medicinal	Light Blue	B.I.M.	2.50-3.50
FITZ SHOE DRESSING FITZ CHEMICAL CO. PHILLIPSBURG, N.J.	5 ½	Shoe Dressing	Aqua	A.B.M.	1.00-1.50
MILANO CARLO ERBA	5 ¾	Unknown	Green	B.I.M.	6.00-8.00

EMBOSSING	HEIGHT	TYPE	COLOR	HOW MADE	PRICE
ONE MINUTE COUGH CURE E. C. DEWITT & CO. CHICAGO. U.S.A.	5 ½	Medicinal	Aqua	B.I.M.	2.00-2.50
THE ABNER ROYCE CO. PURE FRUIT FLAVORS CLEVELAND, O.	5 ⅜	Food	Aqua	B.I.M.	1.50-2.00
NONE	4 ¾	Medicinal	Aqua	B.I.M. Open Pontil Whittle Marked	6.00-8.00
ESTABLISHED 1843-1903 SIXTY YEARS 2 OUNCES FULL MEASURE N. WOOD & SON PORTLAND, ME. (mono as shown)	4 ⅞	Medicinal	Aqua	B.I.M.	1.50-2.00
ZMO FOR PAIN	4 ⅜	Medicinal	Aqua	B.I.M.	1.50-2.00
NATIONAL REMEDY COMPANY NEW YORK	5 ⅜	Medicinal	Aqua	B.I.M.	1.50-2.00
WILLIAMS & CARLETON COMPANY HARTFORD, CONN.	6	Unknown	Aqua	B.I.M.	1.50-2.00
RENNE'S PAINKILLER MAGIC OIL (mono as shown)	6	Medicinal	Light Green	B.I.M.	2.50-3.50

EMBOSSING	HEIGHT	TYPE	COLOR	HOW MADE	PRICE
OMEGA OIL IT'S GREEN THE OMEGA CHEMICAL CO. NEW YORK TRADE MARK (mono as shown)	6 ⅞	Medicinal	Clear	B.I.M.	2.00-2.50
SIROP D'ANIS GAUVIN	5	Unknown	Aqua	B.I.M.	1.50-2.00
on back: GEGENUBER (paper label as shown)	4 ½	Cosmetic	Clear	B.I.M.	2.00-2.50
DERMA-BALM LARKIN CO. BUFFALO DERMA-BALM (paper label as shown)	4 ¾	Cosmetic	Clear	B.I.M.	2.00-2.50
NONE	4 ⅞	Unknown	Aqua	B.I.M.	1.00-1.50
Dr WISTAR'S BALSAM OF WILD CHERRY PHILADa	5	Medicinal	Aqua	B.I.M.	5.00-7.00
CENTAUR LINIMENT	5 ⅛	Medicinal	Aqua	B.I.M. Whittle Marked	2.00-2.50
LARKIN CO. BUFFALO (mono as shown)	5 ½	Cosmetic	Clear	B.I.M. Whittle Marked	2.00-2.50
"WYANOKE" DR. PARK'S INDIAN LINIMENT A. M. FOLLETT, PROP CONCORD, NH	5 ¼	Medicinal	Clear	B.I.M.	2.50-3.50

EMBOSSING	HEIGHT	TYPE	COLOR	HOW MADE	PRICE
DIOS' (pape label as shown) on back: NEUROSINE	6 ¼	Medicinal	Clear	B.I.M.	1.50-2.00
NONE (paper label as shown)	6 ⅛	Food	Clear	B.I.M.	2.00-2.50
(paper label as shown) on back: CARTER GEORGETOWN MASS.	5 ⅛	Extract	Clear	B.I.M.	2.00-2.50
RICHARD HUDNUT NEW YORK (monos as shown) (two R's facing each other on side panels	5 ¾	Cosmetic	Clear	B.I.M. Brass Crown Stopper	2.50-3.50
(paper label as shown) on back: PYRODENT	5 ¾	Medicinal	Clear	B.I.M. Brass Stopper	2.00-2.50
MEXICAN MUSTANG LINIMENT LYON MF'G CO. NEW YORK	5 ½	Medicinal	Aqua	B.I.M.	2.50-3.00
S. O. DUNBAR TAUNTON MASS.	5 ¾	Ink	Aqua	B.I.M.	4.00-6.00

EMBOSSING	HEIGHT	TYPE	COLOR	HOW MADE	PRICE
NONE	5 ¾	Medicinal	Aqua	Free Blown Open Pontil	7.00-9.00
NONE	5 ⅜	Medicinal	Aqua	Free Blown Open Pontil	7.00-9.00
NONE	5 ¼	Medicinal	Aqua	Free Blown Open Pontil	7.00-9.00
NONE	5 ⅛	Medicinal	Aqua	Free Blown Open Pontil	7.00-9.00
NONE	5	Medicinal	Aqua	Free Blown Open Pontil	7.00-9.00
NONE	4 ¾	Medicinal	Aqua	Free Blown Open Pontil	7.00-9.00
NONE	4 ⅝	Medicinal	Aqua	Free Blown Open Pontil	7.00-9.00
NONE	5 ⅜	Medicinal	Aqua	Free Blown Open Pontil	7.00-9.00

EMBOSSING	HEIGHT	TYPE	COLOR	HOW MADE	PRICE
JOHN H PHELPS PHARMACIST PHELPS RHEUMATIC ELIXIR SCRANTON, PA.	5 ½	Medicinal	Aqua	B.I.M.	2.00-2.50
HENRY R. GRAY MONTREAL	5 ¼	Medicinal	Aqua	B.I.M.	1.50-2.00
UNITED STATES MEDICINE CO NEW YORK	5	Medicinal	Aqua	B.I.M.	1.50-2.00
DR MOWE'S COUGH BALSAM LOWELL MASS	4 ⅛	Medicinal	Aqua	B.I.M.	2.00-2.50
HOWE & STEVENS FAMILY DYE COLORS	4	Household	Aqua	B.I.M. Whittle Marked	3.00-4.00
DR E. G. GOULD'S PIN WORM SYRUP	5	Medicinal	Aqua	B.I.M.	2.50-3.50
Dr. H. KELSEY LOWELL MASS	6 ¾	Medicinal	Aqua	B.I.M.	2.50-3.00

EMBOSSING	HEIGHT	TYPE	COLOR	HOW MADE	PRICE
NONE	5 ¾	Whiskey Sampler	Aqua	B.I.M.	2.50-3.00
COLGATE & CO. NEW YORK (mono with C & Co as shown)	5 ½	Cosmetic	Clear	B.I.M.	2.50-3.50
NONE	5 ½	Cosmetic	Clear	B.I.M.	1.50-2.00
CARTER GEORGETOWN MASS.	5 ⅛	Extract	Aqua	B.I.M.	2.00-2.50
NAONI'S CENTAUR LINIMENT KENTARPRE	4 ¾	Medicinal	Aqua	B.I.M.	2.00-2.50
JOHNSON'S AMERICAN ANODYNE LINIMENT	4 ½	Medicinal	Aqua	B.I.M. Whittle Marked Ground Pontil	4.00-6.00
Dr N. C. WHITE'S PULY ELIXIR	4 ½	Medicinal	Aqua	B.I.M.	2.00-2.50
MRS WINSLOW'S SOOTHING SYRUP CURTIS & PERKINS PROPRIETORS	4 ⅞	Medicinal	Aqua	B.I.M. Whittle Marked Ground Pontil	4.00-6.00
NONE	5 ¼	Medicinal	Aqua	Free Blown Open Pontil	7.00-9.00
HEMLOCK OIL CO., WEST DERRY, N.H.	5 ¾	Medicinal	Aqua	B.I.M.	3.00-4.00

EMBOSSING	HEIGHT	TYPE	COLOR	HOW MADE	PRICE
CABOT'S SULPHO-NAPTHOL TRADE MARK REG. U.S. PAT. OFF. BOSTON, MASS. U.S.A.	4 ⅞	Household	Amber Brown	B.I.M.	2.50-3.00
on base: WYETH	4 ½	Medicinal	Amber	B.I.M.	1.50-2.00
on base: BURNETT 13 BOSTON	4 ⅜	Extract	Amber Brown	A.B.M.	1.00-1.50
H. T. & C⁰	4 ⅜	Medicinal	Amber	B.I.M.	2.50-3.00
NONE (paper label as shown)	4 ¾	Medicinal	Amber	B.I.M.	2.50-3.00
NONE (paper label as shown)	4 ⅝	Medicinal	Brown	B.I.M.	2.50-3.00
NONE (paper label as shown)	4 ¾	Medicinal	Amber	B.I.M.	2.50-3.00
METCALF	4 ½	Medicinal	Brown	B.I.M.	2.50-3.00

EMBOSSING	HEIGHT	TYPE	COLOR	HOW MADE	PRICE
KUHN REMEDY CO CHICAGO, ILLS. on base: 1889	4 ⅜	Medicinal	Clear	B.I.M.	1.50-2.00
NONE	4	Medicinal	Clear	Four-Piece Mold Whittle Marked	1.50-2.00
FAIRCHILD'S PEPSIN IN POWDER	4 ⅛	Medicinal	Clear	B.I.M.	1.50-2.00
NONE	5	Medicinal	Aqua	Twelve-Sided Panel Open Pontil Whittle Marked	7.00-9.00
NONE (paper label as shown)	4 ⅞	Medicinal	Aqua	B.I.M.	1.50-2.00
JADWIN'S TAR SYRUP SCRANTON PA.	4 ⅞	Medicinal	Aqua	B.I.M.	1.50-2.00
BECK & CO. BOSTON	4	Medicinal	Clear	B.I.M.	1.50-2.00
J. PETTITS CANKER BALSAM	3 ¼	Medicinal	Aqua	B.I.M. Whittle Marked	2.50-3.50

EMBOSSING	HEIGHT	TYPE	COLOR	HOW MADE	PRICE
PALMER (paper label on neck)	4 ⅝	Perfume	Emerald Green	B.I.M.	6.00-8.00
LYONS POWDER B & P N.Y.	4 ⅜	Cosmetic	Dark Brown	Four-Piece Mold Whittle Marked	4.00-6.00
NONE on base: cross	4	Medicinal	Cobalt Blue	B.I.M.	2.00-3.00
PRESTON OF NEW HAMPSHIRE (when labeled reads: "The Portsmouth Lavender Salt for the Traveller")	3	Smelling Salts	Emerald Green	B.I.M. Glass Stopper	5.00-7.00
NONE	3	Medicinal	Ultra Violet	B.I.M.	4.00-6.00
(mono C & Co as shown)	2 ⅞	Cosmetic	Emerald Green	B.I.M.	3.50-4.50
THE CROWN PERFUMERY COMPANY LONDON	2 ½	Cosmetic	Emerald Green	B.I.M.	3.00-4.00
NONE	4 ½	Medicinal	Dark Violet	B.I.M. Open Pontil Whittle Marked	25.00-35.00
NONE	4 ⅜	Medicinal	Cobalt Blue	A.B.M. Brass Cap	1.50-2.50

EMBOSSING	HEIGHT	TYPE	COLOR	HOW MADE	PRICE
DAVIS' VEGETABLE PAIN KILLER	5	Medicinal	Aqua	B.I.M. Open Pontil Whittle Marked	8.00–10.00
DAVIS' VEGETABLE PAIN KILLER	4 ¾	Medicinal	Aqua	B.I.M.	2.00–2.50
"THREE IN ONE" G. W. COLE CO.	4	Household	Aqua	B.I.M.	1.50–2.00
BAKER'S PURE EXTRACT 2 OUNCES	4 ⅜	Food	S.C.A.	B.I.M.	2.00–2.50
ESTABLISHED 1843 N. WOOD & SON PORTLAND, ME. (mono as shown)	4 ⅝	Medicinal	Clear	B.I.M.	1.50–2.00
INDIAN ROOT BEER EXTRACT	4 ½	Extract	Aqua	B.I.M.	1.50–2.00
GOLTON'S SELECT FLAVOR'S	4 ⅝	Food	Clear	B.I.M.	1.50–2.00
JOHN W. PERKIN'S & CO. PORTLAND ME (mono as shown)	4 ¾	Medicinal	Light Green	B.I.M.	2.00–2.50
NONE	5 ⅛	Medicinal	Aqua	B.I.M.	1.00–1.50

EMBOSSING	HEIGHT	TYPE	COLOR	HOW MADE	PRICE
NONE	5 ⅜	Medicinal	Aqua	B.I.M. Open Pontil Whittle Marked	8.00–10.00
NONE	5 ⅛	Medicinal	Aqua	B.I.M. Open Pontil	7.00–9.00
NONE	4 ⅞	Medicinal	Aqua	B.I.M. Open Pontil Twelve-Sided Panel	7.00–9.00
NONE	4 ¾	Medicinal	Aqua	B.I.M. Open Pontil Whittle Marked	7.00–9.00
NONE	4 ½	Medicinal	Aqua	B.I.M. Open Pontil Whittle Marked Twelve-Sided Panel	8.00–10.00
NONE	5 ½	Medicinal	Aqua	B.I.M. Open Pontil	6.00–8.00
STEPHEN SWEET'S INFALLIBLE LINIMENT	5 ⅛	Medicinal	Aqua	B.I.M. Ground Pontil	6.00–8.00
NONE	5 ⅝	Medicinal	Aqua	B.I.M. Open Pontil Whittle Marked	8.00–10.00

EMBOSSING	HEIGHT	TYPE	COLOR	HOW MADE	PRICE
DOCT MARSHALLS SNUFF (paper label as shown)	3 ½	Medicinal	Aqua	B.I.M.	3.00-4.00
DOCT MARSHALL'S SNUFF	3 ¼	Medicinal	Aqua	B.I.M.	2.50-3.50
DOCT MARSHALL'S CATARRH SNUFF	3 ½	Medicinal	Aqua	B.I.M.	2.50-3.50
DR. WISTAR'S BALSAM OF WILD CHERRY SETH W. FOWLE & SONS BOSTON	3 ½	Medicinal	Light Green	B.I.M.	3.50-4.50
NONE	2 ⅝	Medicinal (Tablets)	Clear	B.I.M.	1.00-1.50
NONE	3 ¼	Medicinal	S.C.A.	B.I.M.	1.50-1.75
NONE	3	Medicinal	Aqua	Free Blown Open Pontil	7.00-9.00
NONE	3	Medicinal	Light Green	B.I.M.	1.50-1.75
(mono as shown with initials MO)	2 ¾	Unknown	Clear	B.I.M.	1.50-2.00
SAMPLE BOTTLE DR. KILMER'S SWAMP-ROOT KIDNEY CURE BINGHAMTON, N.Y.	3 ⅛	Medicinal	Aqua	B.I.M.	3.50-4.50
NONE	3 ⅞	Household (Oil)	Clear	B.I.M.	1.00-1.50

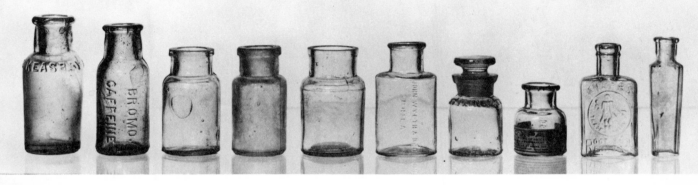

EMBOSSING	HEIGHT	TYPE	COLOR	HOW MADE	PRICE
KEASBEY & MATTISON C. on base: KEASBEY & MATTISON CO D AMBLER, PA.	3 ⅜	Medicinal	Blue	B.I.M.	2.00-2.50
BROMO CAFFEINE	3 ⅛	Medicinal	Blue	B.I.M.	2.00-2.50
NONE	2 ½	Medicinal	Aqua	B.I.M.	1.50-2.00
NONE	2 ⅝	Medicinal	Aqua	B.I.M.	1.50-2.00
NONE	2 ⅝	Medicinal	Aqua	B.I.M. Three-Piece Mold	1.75-2.00
JOHN WYETH & BRO PHILA.	2 ¾	Medicinal	Clear	B.I.M.	1.50-2.00
FORMAN'S ASTRINGENT on base: FORMAN COMPANY N.Y.	2	Medicinal	Clear	B.I.M. Glass Stopper	2.00-2.50
(paper label as shown) on back: DODEZ	1 ¾	Medicinal	Clear	B.I.M.	1.50-2.50
KNAPP'S ROOT BEER EXTRACT (mono as shown with trade mark)	2 ¾	Extract	Light Green	B.I.M.	3.00-4.50
NONE	3	Cologne	Clear	B.I.M.	2.00-2.50

EMBOSSING	HEIGHT	TYPE	COLOR	HOW MADE	PRICE
NONE (paper label as shown)	2 ½	Medicinal	Amber Brown	B.I.M.	2.50-3.00
NONE (paper label as shown)	2 ¾	Medicinal	Amber Brown	B.I.M.	2.50-3.00
(P's as shown)	2 ⅝	Medicinal	Cobalt Blue	B.I.M.	4.00-5.00
(P's as shown)	3	Medicinal	Cobalt Blue	B.I.M.	4.00-6.00
LACTOPEPTINE FOR ALL DIGESTIVE AILMENTS (mono as shown)	2	Medicinal	Teal Green	B.I.M. Screw Threads	5.00-7.00
BROMO-SELTZER EMERSON DRUG CO. BALTIMORE, MD.	2 ½	Medicinal	Cobalt Blue	B.I.M.	2.50-3.00
NONE	3	Medicinal	Amber	B.I.M.	2.00-2.50
NONE	2 ⅞	Medicinal	Amber	B.I.M.	2.00-2.50
HICK'S CAPUDINE FOR HEADACHES	3 ¼	Medicinal	Amber	B.I.M.	2.50-3.00
BELL-ANS FOR INDIGESTION BELL & CO. INC. ORANGEBURG NEW YORK. U.S.A.	2 ⅞	Medicinal	Amber	A.B.M.	1.00-1.50

EMBOSSING	HEIGHT	TYPE	COLOR	HOW MADE	PRICE
NONE	4 ¾	Insulator	Ice Blue		4.00-5.00
NEW ENG. TEL. & TEL. CO.	3 ¾	Insulator	Emerald Green		2.00-3.00
WHITALL TATUM CO. Nº 2 MADE IN U.S.A.	3 ¾	Insulator	Aqua		1.50-2.50
on base: AM INSR CO. PATd SEPT13, 81'	3 ¾	Insulator	Light Green		2.00-3.00
HEMINGRAY - 19 MADE IN U.S.A.	3 ¾	Insulator	Dark Blue		3.00-4.00

EMBOSSING	HEIGHT	TYPE	COLOR	HOW MADE	PRICE
ARMSTRONG'S T.W. MADE IN U.S.A. 12 47	4	Insulator	Clear		1.00-2.00
NEW ENG TEL & TEL CO.	3 ½	Insulator	Emerald Green		2.00-3.00
BROOKFIELD NEW YORK	3 ½	Insulator	Green		3.00-3.50
W. BROOKFIELD NEW YORK	3 ½	Insulator	Aqua		2.50-3.00
NEW ENG TEL & TEL CO	3 ⅝	Insulator	Ice Blue		2.50-3.50

EMBOSSING	HEIGHT	TYPE	COLOR	HOW MADE	PRICE
NONE	2 ⅞	Unknown	Clear	B.I.M. Glass Cap	3.00-4.00
FROST & ADAMS CO BOSTON	3 ⅛	Household (Tooth Powder)	S.C.A.	B.I.M.	2.00-3.00
NONE	2 ¼	Unknown (Possibly Ink)	S.C.A.	B.I.M.	3.00-4.00
NONE	2 ⅝	Cone Ink	Light Blue	B.I.M.	4.50-6.50
on base: CARTER'S 7½ MADE IN U.S.A.	2 ½	Ink	Aqua	B.I.M.	2.00-3.00
CURTIS & BROWN M'F'G. CO. (LIMITED) NEW YORK	3	Medicinal	Clear	B.I.M.	2.50-3.50
NONE	2 ¾	Cosmetic	Clear	B.I.M. Glass Stopper	2.00-2.50

EMBOSSING	HEIGHT	TYPE	COLOR	HOW MADE	PRICE
NONE	5	Medicinal	Aqua	Free Blown Open Pontil	10.00-15.00
NONE	4 ¼	Medicinal	Aqua	B.I.M. Open Pontil Whittle Marked	8.00-10.00
NONE	2 ¼	Umbrella Ink	Deep Green	B.I.M. Open Pontil Whittle Marked	20.00-25.00
NONE	2 ¼	Ink	Clear	B.I.M.	4.00-6.00
W. E. BONNEY (paper label attached to circular area reads: "Bonney's Non Corrosive Ink")	2 ½	Barrel Ink	Aqua	B.I.M.	10.00-14.00
BALSAM OF HONEY	3 ⅝	Medicinal	Light Green	B.I.M. Open Pontil Whittle Marked	8.00-10.00
DR. TOBIAS NEW YORK VENETIAN LINIMENT	4 ¼	Medicinal	Aqua	B.I.M. Whittle Marked Ground Pontil	6.00-8.00

EMBOSSING	HEIGHT	TYPE	COLOR	HOW MADE	PRICE
NONE	2 ½	Cone Ink	Cobalt Blue	B.I.M.	7.00–9.00
NONE	2 ⅞	Umbrella Ink	Aqua	B.I.M.	8.00–10.00
NONE	2 ½	Cone Musilage	Aqua	B.I.M.	4.00–6.00
NONE	2 ¼	Ink	S.C.A.	Turn Mold	6.00–8.00
on base: CARTER'S 7½ MADE IN U.S.A.	2 ¾	Ink	Clear	B.I.M.	2.00–2.50
NONE	3 ⅛	Bell Mucilage	Aqua	B.I.M.	5.00–6.00

Index